Margaret Atwood:
A Feminist Poetics

# Margaret Atwood:

# a

# Feminist Poetics

by Frank Davey

Talonbooks  •  Vancouver  •  1984

Copyright © 1984 Frank Davey

Published with assistance from the Canada Council

TALONBOOKS
201 1019 East Cordova
Vancouver
British Columbia v6a 1m8
Canada

Designed and typeset at The Coach House Press, Toronto
Printed in Canada by Hignell Printing Limited
Second printing: August 1986

CANADIAN CATALOGUING IN PUBLICATION DATA

Davey, Frank, 1940-
Margaret Atwood

(The New Canadian criticism series)
Includes index.
ISBN 0-88922-217-7

1. Atwood, Margaret, 1939- — Criticism and interpretation.
I. Title. II. Series.
PS8501.T89Z63 1984   C813'.54   C84-091453-9
PR9199.3.A88Z63 1984

# Contents

# Abbreviations

Passages from Margaret Atwood's writings have been taken from the following editions:

AC   *The Animals in that Country.*
     Toronto: Oxford University Press, 1968.
BE   *Bluebeard's Egg.* Toronto: McClelland and Stewart, 1983.
BH   *Bodily Harm.* Toronto: McClelland and Stewart, 1981.
CG   *The Circle Game.* Toronto: House of Anansi, 1967.
DG   *Dancing Girls.* Toronto: Seal Books, 1977.
DP   *Double Persephone.* Toronto: Hawkshead Press, 1961.
EW   *The Edible Woman.*
     Toronto: McClelland and Stewart, 1969.
I    *Interlunar.* Toronto: Oxford University Press 1984.
JSM  *The Journals of Susanna Moodie.*
     Toronto: Oxford University Press, 1970.
LO   *Lady Oracle.* Toronto: McClelland and Stewart, 1976.
LBM  *Life Before Man.* Toronto: McClelland and Stewart, 1979.
MD   *Murder in the Dark.*
     Toronto: The Coach House Press, 1983.
PP   *Power Politics.* Toronto: House of Anansi, 1971.
PU   *Procedures for Underground.*
     Toronto: Oxford University Press, 1970.
TS   *True Stories.* Toronto: Oxford University Press, 1981.
THP  *Two-Headed Poems.*
     Toronto: Oxford University Press, 1978.
S    *Surfacing.* Toronto: McClelland and Stewart, 1972.
Su   *Survival.* Toronto: House of Anansi, 1972.
YAH  *You Are Happy.* Toronto: Oxford University Press, 1974.

CHAPTER ONE

# An Unneeded Biography

---

You don't need biographical information unless the work is unintelligible without it. It's most unfortunate that Dorothy Wordsworth kept a diary. I don't care if William Wordsworth *ever* saw a field of golden daffodils.... (Margaret Atwood, Interview with Linda Sandler[1])

MARGARET Atwood was born on the 18th of November, 1939, the second child of Carl Edward Atwood, an entomologist, and Margaret Dorothy Killam. From the time she was six months old until she was eleven, the family spent more than half of each year in the wilderness of Northern Ontario above Temiskaming, where her father conducted research. Atwood describes this period in her article "Travels Back":

Highway 17 was my first highway, I travelled along it six months after I was born, from Ottawa to North Bay and then to Temiskaming, and from there over a one-track dirt road into the bush. After that, twice a year, north when the ice went out, south when the snow came, the time between spent in tents; or in the cabin built by my father on a granite point a mile by water from a Quebec village so remote that the road went in only two years before I was born.[2]

From 1939 to 1945 the family wintered in Ottawa; in 1945 in Sault Ste. Marie, and from 1946 to 1951 in Toronto. Although the remoteness of the family's cabin kept Atwood from completing a full year of school until 1950, it also seems to have made both her early reading and her father's work of special importance to her. The Gothic materials of *Power Politics* and *Lady Oracle,* and the motif of 'miraculous change' which recurs in these books as well as in *Surfacing, The Edible Woman,* and *Procedures for Underground,* can be linked, as she told Linda Sandler, with her childhood reading.

... most fairy tales and religious stories involve miraculous changes of shape. Grimm's tales, Greek and Celtic legends, have them. North American Indian legends have people who are animals in one incarnation, or who can take on the shape of a bird at will. I would say that *Grimm's Fairy Tales* was one of the most influential books I ever read.

References to the biological world of her father's research abound in her work, from the insect-eating sundew and the caterpillars whose metamorphoses form the central images of *Surfacing* and *Lady Oracle* to the "warm rotting of vegetable flesh" in "Pre-Amphibian," the "immigrants" who "danced like sandflies" in "Further Arrivals" and the "dead dog/jubilant with maggots" in "The Double Voice." Atwood discusses this influence with Sandler.

My father is an entomologist and he used to bring home these "things" in one form, they would go through some mysterious process and emerge as something else. So metamorphosis was familiar to me at an early age. Later on I studied chemistry and botany and zoology, and if I hadn't been a writer I'd have gone on with that.[3]

The geography north of Temiskaming must have given Atwood special insight into Susanna Moodie's life in the 1830s in the bush north of Peterborough, and may have provided almost exactly the "lake ... blue and cool as redemption" (S15) at which most of the action of *Surfacing* occurs. She began writing during these childhood years, producing "novels and books of poems" – among them, "a novel about the ant" –

Novels and books of poems, in which I made the book first and filled in the poems later, I was already into publishing. Then I had a sterile period between the age of 9 and the age of 16.... [4]

In the early 1950s Atwood attended Leaside High School in Toronto, where she appears to have been remarkably active. She participated in basketball, the United Nations Club, and a school choral group, and earned the school's citizenship award. Although majoring in Home Economics, in 1955 she began

... writing borderline literary material that people don't usually associate with me – musical comedies, commercial jingles, various things under pseudonyms. I even wrote an opera about synthetic fabrics for my Home Economics class. It was about that time I realized I didn't want to be a home economist, I wanted to be a writer. That was a great change, because I was supposed to be practical and sensible; that was my 'image.'[5]

In her mature writing, this period in Atwood's life appears to be partly metamorphosed into Marian MacAlpin of *The Edible Woman*, a competent homemaker who is burdened with a 'sensible' image (*EW* 89).

Atwood also produced some serious writing during this time – prose modeled on that of Edgar Allan Poe[6] and poetry that "reads like Wordsworth and Lord Byron."[7] Some of this work was published in her school's magazine *Clarion Call*.

It was not until her second or third year at university that Atwood 'discovered' Canadian writing. She had enrolled at Victoria College, University of Toronto, in 1957, and begun studies under Jay Macpherson, Northrop Frye, Kathleen Coburn, and Millar McClure. Her consequent introduction to Canadian books was decisive.

... when I did discover Canadian writing it was a tremendously exciting thing because it meant that people in the country were writing and not only that, they were publishing books. And if they could be publishing books, then so could I. So then I read a lot of stuff, and I was lucky enough to know somebody who had a fairly extensive library of Canadian poetry which I read from beginning to end, so that by the time I was about 21 I had certainly found my tradition.[8]

Her years at Victoria College were active and significant in other ways as well. She participated in dramatic productions, belonged to the debating club, published poetry and prose in the college magazine, *Acta Victoriana*, won the E.J. Pratt medal for her suite of poems "Double Persephone," and began a literary friendship with Dennis Lee who would later be her fellow editor at House of Anansi press. She entered professional publishing with poems in *Canadian Forum, Alphabet, Jargon*, and *Tamarack Review*, and a chapbook edition of "Double Persephone" was produced by John Robert Colombo's Hawkshead Press.

After receiving her BA in Honours English in 1961, Atwood accepted a Woodrow Wilson Fellowship to begin a Masters degree in Victorian literature at Radcliffe College under the Canadian scholar Jerome H. Buckley. She received her MA in 1962 and immediately began doctoral studies. In the fall of 1963 she returned to Toronto and took up work in a market research company – work which was later to serve as field research for Marian MacAlpin's job in *The Edible Woman*. Her first novel, the unpublished *Up in the Air so Blue* was written at this time. She spent 1964-65 in Vancouver as a lecturer in English at the University of British Columbia. During the teaching year she worked on poems later included in *The Circle Game* ("Totems," for example, would appear to be based on the display in the B.C. Provincial Museum in Victoria) and wrote the first draft of *The Edible Woman* the April to August period that followed.

She returned to doctoral study at Harvard in the fall of 1965, completed revision of *The Edible Woman,* and made plans for a thesis on Gothic romance, to be titled "The English Metaphysical Romance." In 1966, her first major poetry collection, *The Circle Game,* was published by Contact Press – to immediate critical praise. In 1967 she won two major Canadian awards: the Centennial Commission Poetry Competition first prize for the poetry suite "The Animals in that Country," and the Governor-General's Award for Poetry for *The Circle Game.* She left Harvard in the summer of 1967 to teach Victorian and American literature at Sir George Williams University in Montreal, and in the fall of 1968 accepted an appointment at the University of Alberta to teach Creative Writing. Rather than completing her thesis, she began work on the poems of *The Journals of Susanna Moodie, Procedures for Underground* (both published in 1970) and *Power Politics* (published in 1971), and also began two novels, one which she abandoned and the second, *Surfacing,* which she completed in August 1970.

With the publication of *The Edible Woman* in 1969 (the manuscript had been misplaced for several years by McClelland & Stewart) and the sale of its film rights for $15,000, Atwood was able to spend 1970-71 in Toronto, England, France, and Italy. These European travels would later inform her novel *Lady Oracle* and short story "The Grave of the Famous Poet." In 1972-73 she accepted a one-year appointment to teach in the Humanities Division of York University. One of her assignments here, fortuitously, was to teach a Canadian culture course with Eli Mandel; her lecture notes for this course became *Survival: a Thematic Guide to English-Canadian Literature* – the most controversial and widely-selling Canadian literary title of 1972. *Surfacing* was also published that year.

By the end of 1972, with five major collections of poetry, two novels, and one book of criticism published and critically well-received, Atwood had become one of the most sudden literary successes in Canadian history. In less than six years she had gone from the obscurity of occasional publication in *Alphabet* and *The Canadian*

*Forum* to the notoriety of newspaper features[9] and a cover story in *Saturday Night*.[10] The notoriety – particularly the attempts of several journalists to stereotype or mythologize her – was not at all welcome to Atwood, whose work, if anything, argued for the demythologizing of women. In an April 1973 speech to the Empire Club she observed that she was becoming a symbol of Canadian cultural aspirations, a 'thing' rather than merely a celebrity.[11] Somewhat later she exclaimed,

I don't particularly like being a public figure. It's not something I set out to do, it's something I found happening to me. I was quite unprepared, and rather horrified by some of the results.[12]

Still later, to another interviewer, Atwood suggested that her public image had become the psychological projection of her readers' wishes and fears.

The public has given me a personality of not having a public personality. Sometimes they make up things about it like Margaret the Monster, Margaret the Magician and Margaret the Mother – Romantic notions of what's really there keep getting in the way of people's actual view of you.[13]

One is reminded here of how Atwood portrayed Peter in *The Edible Woman* as able to see Marian only as the stereotyped embodiment of the fiancée he desires, or Joan in *Lady Oracle* as projecting onto all men the image of her killer / healer father.

Despite this problem of public image, the subsequent years have been productive ones for Atwood. Her work since 1973 has included the CBC Television play *The Servant Girl* (1974), the poetry collections *You Are Happy* (1974), *Two-Headed Poems* (1980), *True Stories* (1981), and *Interlunar* (1984), the novels *Lady Oracle* (1976), *Life Before Man* (1979), and *Bodily Harm* (1981), the short story collections *Dancing Girls* (1977) and *Bluebeard's Egg* (1983), the book of "short fictions and prose poems" *Murder in the Dark* (1983), the children's book *Up in the Tree* (1978), the history book *Days of the Rebels: 1815-1840* (1977), and the essay collection *Second Words* (1982). She has been awarded honorary doctorates by Trent and Queen's universities and the University of Toronto, served as Writer-in-Residence at the University of Toronto, won the Bess Hopkins Prize from *Poetry (Chicago)*, won the City of Toronto Book Award for *Lady Oracle*, won the St. Lawrence University Prize (given to the best first collection of short fiction by a North

American) for *Dancing Girls,* and won the 1982 Welsh Arts Council International Writer's Prize. In addition, she served on the Board of Directors of the Canadian Civil Liberties Association from 1973 to 1975, and on the editorial board of House of Anansi Press from 1971 to 1973. Although not a founding member of this nationalist press, she played an important and often unpaid role in its surviving a "whirlpool"[14] of crises and conflicts in this period. Atwood currently lives in Toronto with novelist Graeme Gibson and their daughter Jess.

*

These biographical details do not explain Atwood's writing; they are merely – as we might expect – consistent with it. The numerous parallels between her life and her writing – her work in market research and Marian MacAlpin's job with Seymour Surveys, her parent's Temiskaming cabin and the setting of *Surfacing,* her having once worked at the archery range of a Toronto Sportsmen's Show and Joan Foster's similar job in *Lady Oracle* – are much less significant than the fictional structures which she builds around them. A writer inevitably begins with her own experience; in Atwood's case the final result often appears to be fictionalized versions of the original experience, fictionalized Atwoods, hypothetical selves whose reality lies in the fictional vision rather than in the auto-biographical materials which gave rise to them.

It's been a constant interest of mine: change from one state to another, change from one thing into another.[15]

An in-depth biographical study of Atwood will eventually be needed, not to explain her work but to demythologize it, to free it of its "Margaret the Mother" or "Margaret the Monster" associations by making clear the specific and actual of her private life. In fact, it may be the lack of autobiographical specificity in her early poetry, its distancing of the personal, that has stimulated autobiographical speculation. The voice of many of the poems of *The Circle Game* is a dramatic voice; it speaks to other characters in the poems rather than to the reader, particularly in the title poem. The reader overhears her words, rather than having them addressed to him. In *Power Politics* the third-person titles of the poems ("They Eat Out," "She Considers Evading Him") further distance the speaker while her second-person addresses to her lover place the reader in the role of eavesdropper. In these books and in *The Journals of Susanna Moodie,* Atwood creates

personae, masks, to speak for her. The central fact about a mask is
that it hides. Why is a mask being used, the reader wonders. What
does it conceal? More specifically, what is she hiding? In later poems
where Atwood appears to drop the mask and speak directly from the
autobiographical backdrop of her Alliston farm or her daughter Jess
("The Bus to Alliston, Ontario," *THP* 76-78, "Spelling," *TS* 63-64)
the power of the poem to stimulate biographical speculation seems
to diminish, possibly because the biographical is no longer mysterious.

*

Eli Mandel, of course, feels that all works of criticism are novels, and in a
way he's right. They *are* imaginative constructs.[16]

Atwood's recurrent use of personae in these early poems means
that the critic can never be sure that Atwood is speaking in her own
voice (i.e. out of her own biography or beliefs) and wishes to be held
responsible for the implications of a given statement or image. In
some cases he cannot be sure of the sex of the speaker. Spoken in the
dramatic context of *Power Politics,* "The sun doesn't forgive, / it
looks and keeps going." is a relative statement which provides information chiefly about its speaker. In the poem "Christmas Carols" of
*True Stories,* however, is the statement "Children do not always
mean / hope. To some they mean despair" to be taken as Atwood's
own statement or that of an unsignalled persona? To confuse matters
further, this poem is contained in a collection entitled 'true stories.'
"Don't ask for the true story," the voice of the title poem (or the historical Atwood) advises, "why do you need it?"

Criticism, of course, is not any more a 'true story' than is an
Atwood poem or novel. Nor should it be a fantasy. Like the writer's
work, it is a fiction built on facts, a fiction believed by the critic, to be
a 'probable fiction.' Particularly in the case of a writer as elusive and
playful as Atwood, a critic is left to extrapolate and hypothesize – in
the present book to 'fictionalize' that, unless otherwise indicated, the
voice of an Atwood poem is female, that unless clearly bracketed by
dramatic context, a poem speaks to us – or tricks us – in the poet's
personal voice.

# CHAPTER TWO

# Poetry of Male and Female Space

---

"Plato / has a lot to answer for."
("Sunset I," *TS* 80)

IN "Formal Garden," the opening poem of Margaret Atwood's first book, *Double Persephone*, a

> ... girl with the gorgon touch
> Stretches a glad hand to each
> New piper peddling beds of roses
> Hoping to find within her reach
>
> At last, a living wrist and arm
> Petals that will crush and fade
> But always she meets a marbled flesh
> a fixing eye, a stiffened form
> Where leaves turn spears along the glade.

The girl has a life-arresting "gorgon touch," the poem tells us, but can we believe this? Elsewhere, the poem's language questions whether this touch is intrinsically hers or merely assigned to her by the "pipers" she encounters in this strange garden. Like all the poems in *Double Persephone*, "Formal Garden" is a pastoral, and thereby part of one of the inherited time-freezing ("gorgonesque," we might say) modes of Western literature. But while the "piper" is an expected figure in a pastoral, "girl" is not; the expected female figures are "nymph" or "shepherdess." "Girl" is a temporal term, "piper" atemporal. The girl's "gorgon touch" is contradicted by her "glad hand" and by her "hoping" for the clearly temporal "petals that will crush and fade." It is the piper who has the truly gorgonesque qualities – "marble flesh, a fixing eye, a stiffened form."

There is an Alice-in-Wonderland quality to the girl's experience here. She is very much in foreign territory – a living being in a timeless garden. Bewildered by its formal postures, she causelessly blames herself for them, assigns to her "glad hand" the "gorgon touch." Flesh-and-blood girl in the timeless ceremonial garden of patriarchal mythology: this is a basic dramatic situation in Margaret Atwood's writing. It underlies the male-female relationships in the novels and long poems, and forms an essential part of her political, social and aesthetic stances. In this early poem the several binary oppositions involved in these stances are already evident: between life and artifice, between actuality and inherited mythology, between biology and technology. The life-affirming "glad hand" meets the artifice of the statue's "all-too-perfect grace"; the biological inevitability of "petals that will crush and fade" encounters biology transformed into technology where "leaves turn [into] spears."

*

The white king moves
by memories and procedures
and corners
no final ending but
a stalemate,
forcing her universe
to his geographies
("An Attempted Solution for Chess Problems," CG 18)

Perhaps the most pervasive element in Margaret Atwood's poetry is its sense of male and female space. Male space is not merely inherited, defined by "memories and procedures," but in *The Circle Game* and after is mathematical, imposes "ruled squares on the green landscape" (CG 18). Female space is its Other – the "girl" who must be fitted into the pastoral conventions, the "green landscape" that must yield to chessboard pattern. Male space is substantial, ostensibly unchanging; female space is insubstantial, anonymous, subject to time, and often expressed as organic matter.

Love, you must choose
Between two immortalities:
One of earth, lake, trees
Feathers of a nameless bird
The other of a world of glass
Hard marble, carven word
(DP [13])

In *Power Politics* male space is metallic, sculptural – "a fish hook" – and to the woman's "open eye" (*PP* 1) appears lethal; such space is expressed both in Atwood's characterization of the man and in the predictable, patterned relationship he seeks.

Your face is silver
and flat, scaled like a fish

The death you bring me
is curved, it is in the shape
of door knobs, moons,
glass paperweights

Male energy here has even transformed the traditional spherical 'moon' image of the female into the instrumental and closed shapes of doorknob and paperweight. The latter has become an imprisoning pattern of weddingcake sculpture.

Inside it, snow and lethal
flakes of gold fall endlessly
over an ornamental scene
a man and woman, hands joined and running
(*Power Politics*, 56)

It is enclosing male space which the pioneer of "The Progressive Insanities of the Pioneer" attempts to "impose ... with shovels" on the Canadian landscape. The landscape itself is female, and occupies a role parallel to that of the woman in *Power Politics*. It replies to his phallic egocentric violence with its own anonymous and organic silence.

He asserted
into the furrows, I
am not random

The ground
replied with aphorisms,

a tree-sprout, a nameless
weed, words
he couldn't understand.
(*AC* 36)

*

Technology and mythology are the two major male sources of power
in Atwood's poetry, both because they assert the priority of space
over time. It is technology – measurement, instrumentation – that
the pioneer attempts to use against the land when he paces off his
fields and wields his shovel, hoping to arrest the "surf of undergrowth" and "the swamp's clamourings." It is technology that has
taken the Indian totem poles of "Totems" out of time ("uprooted"
them both from the earth and from the culture which created them)
and inserted them into the "static" space of museum display. Here
Atwood contrasts a neglected "real" pole which has temporal "life in
the progressing / of old wood back to / the earth" with not only the
technologically restored poles (the "wooden people") but with
"tourists" ("other wooden people") who pose "for each other's
cameras"(CG 59-60).

The camera, an overtly time-fixing instrument, is a frequent symbol in Atwood's writing for the conversion of female space into male.
The Atwood photographer is usually male, the person photographed
female, so that both technology and spatial design remain "male" by
association and time and natural process "female." The poem
"Camera" (CG 45-46) presents a "camera man" who in his quest for
an "organized instant" wants all reality – including the implicitly
female voice of the poem – to "stop," "hold still."

you make me stop walking
and compose me on the lawn;

you insist
that the clouds stop moving
the wind stop swaying the church
on its boggy foundations
the sun hold still in the sky
(CG 45)

His subject, however, insists in replying that the spatial object which
the camera creates is itself subject to temporality.

Wherever you partly are
now, look again
at your souvenir,
your glossy square of paper
before it dissolves completely
(CG 46)

Despite the time-fixing and light-fixing act of photography, historical time moves at "the speed of light" to decompose both the photograph and the objects the camera man hoped to save from time; ultimately the church will be reduced to "a pile of muddy rubble / in the
foreground" and the woman subject to a "small black speck / travelling towards the horizon / at almost the speed of light" (CG 45-46).
Throughout the poem Atwood organizes its objects into opposing
polar clusters: on the one side the man, his camera, and his "square
of paper," on the other the woman speaker, the clouds, the sun, the
church on its "boggy foundations," the dissolving force of time.

    Two other poems use photographs with dissolving subjects to
argue the artificiality of the time-fixing technological view of experience, although neither clearly associates this view with the male.
However, in each poem, "This is a Photograph of Me" and "Girl and
Horse, 1928," the subject who evades and disproves photography's
"organized instant" is a woman. In "This is a Photograph of Me" a
"drowned" narrator claims to be "in the lake, under the center / of
the picture, just under the surface" – presumably under the surface of
both the lake and the photo. Her appearance in the photograph is
not, as we expect, a spatial phenomenon; it takes place in time – "if
you look long enough eventually / you will be able to see me" (CG
11). Temporality lurks, the poem argues, under the deceptively solid
surfaces of human creations. In "Girl and Horse, 1928" the voice of
the poem speaks from outside the photo to its girl-subject, insisting
that her smile and pastoral surroundings are illusory.

Why do you smile? Can't you
see the apple blossoms falling around
you, snow, sun, snow,
listen, the tree
dies and is being burnt

Like the formal garden of Double Persephone, the photographic illusion is attractive, but in actuality the "instant" of the photo ceased
even as the shutter closed.

(on the other side
of the picture, the instant
is over, the shadow
of the tree has moved. You wave,

then turn and ride
out of sight through the vanished
orchard.... (PU 10)

Again the objects in these poems occur as parts of a binary opposition. In "This is a Photograph of Me," surface is opposed by subsurface, solid by liquid; in "Girl and Horse, 1928" the surface of the photo is opposed by its "other side," the girl's "smile" by her "wave," the "tree" by the "vanished orchard," the poem's first four stanzas by its last two parenthetical ones. The temporal side of the opposition is again associated with the persona of the poems, and with the girl who by merely riding away defeats the camera's glass eye.

*

As we read through Margaret Atwood's collections of poetry, we find her building a catalogue of the methods by which mankind attempts to affirm male space over female space, to affirm the conviction that "nothing can change." All methods involve a denial of temporality. One is classical mythology – the formal gardens of *Double Persephone* and of "Circe / Mud Poems" in *You Are Happy* – a mythology which, as Robert Graves and Sir James Frazer have suggested, is likely a Bronze Age patriarchal displacement of the mostly female deities of an earlier matriarchal culture.[1] Another is popular mythology, which mimics the classical in its portrayal of male heroes and female handmaidens, the archetypal pattern embodied by both Jason and Medea and Superman and Lois Lane. Thus Atwood's "Superman" portrayal of the man in "They Eat Out" (*PP* 5-6) her comicbook heroes wearing "rubber suits" in "Comic Books vs. History" (*PU* 48-49), or her "starspangled cowboy" with "porcelain grin" of "Background Addresses Cowboy" (*AC* 50-51). Closely related to these is popular entertainment, formulaic, "endless," "stale":

You take my hand and
I'm suddenly in a bad movie,
it goes on and
why am I fascinated

We waltz in slow motion
through an air stale with aphorisms
we meet behind endless potted palms
you climb through the wrong windows.   (*PP* 3)

The third means of denying time, technology, has been gradually expanded by Atwood from the camera, blueprint ("The City

Planners," *CG*11), and the museum ("A Night in the Royal Ontario Museum, *AC* 20-21) of her early books to the more explicitly violent electrodes, motors, and "common pin" of poems like "The Arrest of the Stockbroker."

And the union leader with electrodes
clipped to the more florid
parts of his body, wired like
an odd zoological diagram:
if you don't keep your mouth shut
they'll choose the noise
you emit ...
.... Reading the papers, you've seen it all:
the device for tearing out fingernails,
the motors, the accessories,
what can done with the common pin.
Not to mention the wives and children.
(*TS* 48)

*

A part of all the above is the philosophic strategy of humanism, the strategy of Atwood's pioneer who asserts man's timeless centrality in a Heraclitean nature palpably without centres. The poem, "Progressive Insanities of a Pioneer" contains Atwood's most vivid portrait of the humanist.

He stood, a point
on a sheet of green paper
proclaiming himself the centre,

with no walls, no borders
anywhere; the sky no height
above him, totally un-
enclosed
and shouted:

Let me out!
(*AC* 36)

Throughout the poem the pioneer's sensibilities are governed by artificially defined space; he is appalled by the absence of walls and borders, he creates a house, fences, furrows, in stubborn resistance to the fact that "unstructured space is a deluge." He attempts the Adamic act of naming the objects in his environment – to use language's abstracting power to lift them out of time and into the categories of rationalism. (Adam, of course, is the oldest patriarch of all, and source of one of the most enduring European myths of male primacy.) However, in Atwood the Adamic giving of names fails, nature refuses to receive, refuses, we might say, the traditional female role.

Things
refused to name themselves, refused
to let him name them.

Ultimately, female space – space that exists in time – prevails. The "unnamed whale" of process bursts through his fences, his fields, his clearings, and his subject-object categorizing mind. By implication, purely spatial aesthetics, the humanist ordering of space, and the patriarchal myth of the hero who conquers disorder are also discredited. The land here is metaphorically both female and primitive. It is the raw material of art and of sexual relationship. The pioneer resembles the artist-lover of *Double Persephone* who must choose between "earth lake trees" and the less challenging and fulfilling "world of glass, hard marble, carven word" (*DP* 13).

*

*The Journals of Susanna Moodie* narrates yet another struggle between female and male space. The theme is signalled in the opening poem when Mrs. Moodie, loyal product of eighteenth-century English paternalism, laments that "the moving water will not show me my reflection." She sees her adversaries as the sun ("The Planters," 16-17), change ("The Wereman," 19), unpredictability ("First Neighbours," 14-15), and "fire" – both literal fire and the "fire" of seasonal process ("The Two Fires," 22-23). Much like the pioneer, she covets security and stability; she attempts to achieve these through his time-denying strategies of categorization, measurement and enclosure.

... concentrate on
form, geometry, the human
architecture of the house, square
closed doors, proved roofbeams,
the logic of windows. (22)

But the "white chaos" (23) of her new environment continually forces itself upon her as the only reality. Whiteness and light, frequent images in Atwood for camera-defying cosmic energy, surround and absorb her. A photograph taken in her old age ironically documents her temporality rather than fixing it.

I orbit
the apple trees
white white spinning
stars around me

I am being
eaten away by light.
("Daguerreotype Taken in Old Age," 48)

Susanna Moodie's death removes her from all possibility of the spatial illusion – from walls, manners, categorizations, clichés "set up ... at intervals" (55 – Atwood puns here on the Latin *inter vallum*, "between walls"). It confronts her with raw process – here, as elsewhere in Atwood, metaphorically termed "underground." "Underground" for Mrs. Moodie is a "blizzard," a "whirlwind," "a holy fire" ("Resurrection," 58-59). It moves her in the last lines of the book to declare war on conventional spatial structure and location.

I am the old woman
sitting across from you on the bus,
...
out of her eyes come secret
hatpins, destroying
the walls, the ceiling

Turn, look down:
there is no city;
this is the centre of a forest

your place is empty
("A Bus along St Clair: December," 61)

*

Imagery of "underground" is one of Atwood's most important signs throughout her poetry for asserting the dominance of temporally active space over static space, of the female over the male. Like the ghost of Mrs. Moodie, time and process are subversive; they lurk under the surfaces of lakes and photographs, under the ostensibly solid veneers of field, wall, and street. Process is liquid; substantiality – the basis of static form – is an illusion which Adamic men have invented through their fences and their camera-eyes. Mrs. Moodie calls Canada a "land I floated on / but could not touch to claim" (30). The pioneer declares

> The land is solid
> and stamped
>
> watching his foot sink
> down through stone
> up to the knee (AC 36)

Appearances are thus duplicitous: the appearance of stasis conceals process; the appearance of solidity conceals liquidity; the appearance of predictability presages surprise. The double condition of "double" Persephone, desiring process but receiving stone, is reversed for many of Atwood's later female protagonists. The doubleness of reality for them lies in invisibly temporal reality embedded in ostensibly spatial objects. This doubleness requires a "double voice," one with "manners" for the man-made world, and one with "knowledge" for its other ("The Double Voice," JSM 42), or mastery of "procedures for underground." Time-transcending devices – mythology, art, rationalism, stylization – must be recognized as either weapons or crutches used by the weak in the face of mutability. The weak are usually male – the pioneer, Mr. Moodie, the lover in Power Politics, the "camera man," the "piper."

Many Atwood poems imply a female persona who gives herself with zestful ironic self-awareness to games, poses, mythologies, and sculptural perceptions.

> We sit at a clean table
> eating thoughts from clean plates
>
> and see, there is my heart
> germfree, and transparent as glass
>
> and there is my brain, pure
> as cold water in the china
> bowl of my skull.
> ("A Meal," CG 33)

These women are, like Mrs. Moodie, subversives. While living within the male architecture of walls, tables, cleanliness, and glass, their loyalties are to another realm of decay, growth, and organic change. Their poems are like "notes from the underground," as above, where the speaker mocks values she has only pretended to embrace.

*

The persona of *Power Politics* has this kind of ironic awareness of her participation in the masculine "circle game." Her lover is another of the men of stone Atwood's "gorgon" personae, especially in the early poems, tend to encounter.

You stay closed, your skin
is buttoned firmly around you,
your mouth is a tin decoration,
you are in the worst possible taste.

You are as fake as the marble trim
around the fireplace ... (44)

Some of this man's determined attempts to transcend time involve commercial mythology – "suspended above the city / in blue tights and a red cape / eyes flashing in unison"; some involve political mythology.

in a year there will be nothing left
of you but a megaphone

or you will descend through the roof
with the spurious authority of a
government official
blue as a policeman, grey as a used angel. (30)

His beloved enters only sardonically into his spatial assumptions about the world. For her they constitute play; for him they are totally serious.

Put down the target of me
you guard inside your binoculars,
in turn I will surrender

this aerial photograph
(your vulnerable
sections marked in red)
I have found so useful. (37)

Much of the charm of this book resides in the woman's mocking use of the man's spatial assumptions and in the playfulness of her acceptance of a mutually exploitive relationship. He wishes to be a statue; she treats him like one. He acts insensitively; she parodies his insensitivity with a gambit of her own.

I approach this love
like a biologist
putting on my rubber:
gloves and white labcoat
....
Please die, I said
so I can write about it. (10)

Here again a doubleness is posited. Games are sterile but entertaining; statues are cold but beautiful, order is illusory but addictive; the game of love is exhilarating but not loving. Beneath these various paradoxes lurks the central one of space subverted by time, the man parodied by the woman. "Power politics" for the persona is a children's game of pretense and fantasy. The verbal wit of the book suggests the excitement of gamesmanship, not the passions of anger or regret. The persona's ironic role playing suggests both the double vision of Susanna Moodie and a duplicitous 'procedure' for survival in a male environment.

*

A considerable change occurs in Atwood's depiction of male versus female space in the late 1970s. The mood of the poem becomes darker, its violence more intense and literal, the subject matter more overtly political. Atwood's poetry has always managed to transcend the personal to attain cultural relevance; the lovers of "The Circle Game" and *Power Politics* are all simultaneously individual and generic figures. But in *Two Headed Poems* (1977), *True Stories* (1981) and *Murder in the Dark* (1983) the violence changes from the psychological abuses of *Power Politics* or the ecological violations of "Progressive Insanities" to torture, rape, mutilation, and political murder. Again the agent of violence is male.

Cowboy boots, two of them, planted apart, stomp, stomp on main street just before the shot rings out. A spur, in the groin. A man's gotta do, but why this? Jackboots, so highly shined you can see your face in the right one, as the left one raises itself and the heel comes down on your nose. Now you see rows of them marching, marching; yours in the street-level view, because you are lying down. Power is the power to smash, two hold your legs, two your arms, the fifth shoves a pointed instrument into you; a bayonet, the neck of a broken bottle, and it's not even wartime, this is a park, with a children's playground, tiny red and yellow horses, it's daytime, men and women stare at you out of their closed car windows. Later the policeman will ask you what you did to provoke this. ("Liking Men," *MD* 54)

Structurally, this is the same violent scene that Atwood has presented many times in her poetry, the "power mower / cutting a straight swath in the discouraged grass" ("The City Planners," *CG* 27), the camera that stops the clouds ("Camera," *CG* 45), the fish-hook in the open eye (*PP* 1). Semantically, however, it is new; the violence is actual rather than symptomatic, the violent terms are denotative rather than symbolic or metaphoric. While the earlier poems could be read as assigning blame to a culture, "Liking Men" demands to be read as blaming individual men.

This overt identification of the time-resisting impulse as being factually as well as metaphorically male occurs first in *Two-Headed Poems,* in "Marrying the Hangman," Atwood's cryptic retelling of the story of how in 1751 a young Quebec servant girl could escape execution only by marrying the official hangman. Atwood writes this poem in prose, as if to emphasize that this woman's situation is no mere metaphor, no literary device, but actual. She begins it with a differentiation between man and woman, and with an insistence on the story's factuality.

She has been condemned to death by hanging. A man may escape death by becoming the hangman, a woman by marrying the hangman. But at the present time there is no hangman; thus there is no escape. There is only a death, indefinitely postponed. This is not fantasy, this is history.

Three times in the narrative Atwood will repeat that the story is "history." Midway through the poem Atwood interpolates a vague but suggestive passage about two woman friends who appear to have been assaulted by men. The effect of this passage, which is tied linguistically to the main story both by its rhythm and by its concluding "this is not fantasy, this is history, there is more than one hangman," is to generalize the 1751 tale. The hangman, who is "not such a bad fellow," who wants "only the simple things," becomes average man; the condemned woman becomes all women whose lives have required some compromise with men, some "marriage" to the hangman.

At the end of the poem Atwood makes male-female distinctions that reach back through all her work.

He said: food, boot, order, city, fist, roads, time, knife. She said, water, night, willow, rope hair, earth belly, cave, meat, shroud, open, blood. (*THP* 48-51)

For him *foot,* unit of measurement, *boot,* to separate the human body from earth, *order,* to arrest process, *city,* to conceal earth, *fist,* to assert human will, *roads,* to rationalize space, *time,* to measure and control process, *knife,* to assert will, to stop process, to objectify meat. For her *water,* protean, unshapeable, *night,* unilluminated, *willow,* the water tree, *rope hair, earth belly, cave, meat, shroud, blood* – primitive, biological, flesh joined to earth. In these distinctions Atwood's recurrent concerns with feminism and ecology merge. Woman's body is also the world's body; the male desire to have woman mirror back to him his own needs (see "Tricks with Mirrors," *YAH* 24-27) is merely another form of the humanistic male will to have the planet mirror back his utilitarian purposes. ('Mirror,' like 'knife' and 'road' here, becomes throughout Atwood's work a male image, counter to the both reflecting and opening 'water' of the condemned woman.)

The sexual dichotomy of "Marrying the Hangman" returns us to the architecture versus blizzard opposition of *The Journals of Susanna Moodie,* the glass versus earth opposition of *Double Persephone,* the "that country" versus "this country" opposition of *The Animals in that Country,* and invests each of these with sexual meaning. It reaches ahead also to the political poems of *Two-Headed Poems* and *True Stories* in which the world's torturers and oppressors are associated with masculine images of knives and technology and their victims with feminine ones of earth and flesh. The traditional male-female opposition between sun-father and earth-mother, between reason and intuition, sun and moon, Apollo and Artemis, lurks beneath Atwood's imagery here, as in "The Right Hand Fights with the Left." In this poem war begins when

... the right hand dips down
into the chemicals of its own blood
and comes up metal.

It arranges the nouns it has killed
in plaza windows,
....
It oils itself and makes lists
of its enemies, it swivels
on the wrist like a spy, a radar,
a tentacled silver eye.

Arrangement, calculation, and analysis in the right hand cause the left, which is revealingly "soft and smaller," to "at sunset" call out

Arise, O fingers
of the left hand, and outside, in a tangle
of liquid roots and the quick sprawl
of tendrils over the earth,
the forces of the left hand wake
to savage life

The "liquid roots" here evoke the numerous drowned landscapes and subterranean waters of Atwood's writing – the "clamouring swamps" of "Progressive Insanities," the earth as "acid sea" of "Daybooks II" (*THP* 97), the "seared meadows" and "swamps" of "Totems," the everpresent "leaking boat" (*THP* 27) of temporal process.

*

Clearly both the left hand and right are violent. The difference between them lies in the kind of consciousness that underlies the violence; the right hand acts malevolently, the left savagely, preconsciously. This is a concept Atwood clarifies in *True Stories,* in "Landcrab I," "Landcrab II" and "Trainride, Vienna-Bonn." In the landcrab poems Atwood locates the female crab in the familiar dichotomy of man-made order versus water. The crab's world is the beach, its food "soaked nuts, waterlogged sacks ... soggy chips and crusts." The world the poem's human speaker returns to is a fixed one – "moored boats ... blue lights of the dock." But "a piece of what we are" resides in this simple amoral "mouth on stilts."

The truth is we were born
from stones, dragons, the sea's
teeth, as you testify,
with your crest and jagged scissors

the speaker (transforming into evolutionary terms the Greek legend
of Cadmus and the dragon's teeth) says to the crab.

It is a similar primitive violence that Atwood envisions in "Trainride, Vienna-Bonn," when figures in the Black Forest outside the
train window trigger in her mind images of the casual murders of
Fascist Germany.

This forest is alive
to me, closer than skin
unknown, something early
as caves and burned hair,

a chipped stone knife, the
long bone lying in darkness
inside my right arm: not
innocent but latent.
(*TS* 62)

The argument that is implicit but unstated in this poem is that the
deliberate male violence of murder and torture is an extension of a
primitive realm only the female has retained access to; that the masculine realm of order, boot and glass has made itself powerless to
resist enacting this violence because of its refusal to acknowledge the
"long bone" of the primitive that lies "latent" within it. In basic outline, this is a Freudian argument in which female id is repressed by
masculine superego, and in which only a cathartic acknowledgment
of id can restore the healthy state of integration which once pre-
vailed.

Why should there be a war?
Once there was none.

The left hand sang the rituals,
the right hand answered.
("The Right Hand Fights against the Left," *THP* 56)

*

But there has been no catharsis. The most brutal phases of a "war of the body against itself" (*THP* 57) are the rapes, mutilations and forced prostitutions of "A Woman's Issue," a poem which leads Atwood to envision the female genitals as an invaded and desecrated landscape, reminiscent of the farm in "Progressive Insanities of a Pioneer."

... in between the legs,
....
Enemy territory, no man's
land, to be entered furtively
fenced, owned but never surely.

What follows is a horrific view of male approaches to woman — "desperate forays / at midnight, captures / and sticky murders, doctors' rubber gloves, / greasy with blood" — in which man's ultimate weapon is "the word *love*" (*TS* 55). The utter estrangement between the sexes is such that in a slightly later poem, "Him,"

... when you open the door to him, it's ... as if he's just come from another planet, he stands there semi-blinded, by the sudden light, as if you are shedding it, from within, as if he is his own dark hurtling gravity-free interior and he's just landed and you are the land. ....
How many times have you awakened in the moonlight and seen those indigo shadows instead of eyes, hard as if cast by granite, and thought, I'm in bed with a killer. (*MD* 56)

Yet despite such deep estrangement, some reconciliation or catharsis must take place. Accompanying all Atwood's recent accounts of the female abused by male are overtures of hope (the speaker in "Him" says "*I come in peace* you want to prompt him, but don't. He's anxious enough already.") and declarations of the necessity of a sexual truce.

In this furious chase
....
there is no winner, only joy
and no joy.
("The Right Hand Fights against the Left," *THP* 56)

Isn't this the man through whom all men can be forgiven? Must be forgiven, because now you're beginning to remember the way the others were partly like him. ("Him," *MD* 56)

Even the best men are "right-handed" in Atwood's view, admire "well played games" ("Him"), wish "furniture, flowers," and "her arranged just so.... For contemplation and disposition of parts to compose a unified and aesthetic whole" ("Iconography," *MD* 52). Whether involved with human relationships or the natural environment, they prefer the formal garden to the "swamp's clamourings." Simultaneously dangerous and pathetic, they approach the female bearing their "sadness like a clumsy plumber's wrench, a tool for bludgeoning water" ("Him").

*

The usual male analysis of the opposition in Western culture between an organic and an instrumental view of experience posits a dramatic change from the former to the latter in the sixteenth century. To social historians like R.L. Tawney in *Religion and the Rise of Capitalism*,[2] the major signs of this change are the Protestant Reformation, the emergence of a mercantile 'middle' class, and the secularization of values which this class created. To Ian Watt, who in *The Rise of the Novel*[3] locates the origin of the novel partly in this new middle class's desire to learn 'correct' social behavior, this cultural shift is marked by, among other things, an interest in the practical value of realistic fiction – its utility in teaching social decorum and in validating the materialism of the new class. Karl Jaspers in *Man in the Modern Age* describes this cultural change by arguing that for medieval 'man' "history was supernatural ... this world in its immanence ... [was] substantially unhistorical.... But when this transcendent outlook was changed into ... one in which the world was regarded as a movement, as an immanent progression, there awakened a consciousness in men's minds that their own epoch was somehow different from all that had preceded it, and ... that – perhaps ... through purposive effort on their part – something distinctive would grow out of it."

From the sixteenth century onward, there was no break in the continuity of the chain thanks to which, as generation followed generation, link after link passed on the consciousness of the epoch from one generation to another.

This continuity began with the deliberate secularization of human life.
....

... the new astronomy was born, modern science began, the great era of technique was dawning; the State administrations were being nationalized. The idea of progress was conceived.... Whereas hitherto when men had looked forward it had been to the end of the world and the Judgement Day, they now contemplated the perfectionment of civilisation.[4]

It is a similar view of Western history that lies behind Irving Layton's intermittent condemnations of the "rationalists and secularists among us," of "gimmickry," "technique," "rationalizing intellect," "facts and logic" in poetry, and his calling for writing that is "marvellous" and "prophetic."[5]

Reason, intelligence, craftsmanship are things everyone feels more at home with, more particularly Canadians who are likely to feel bewildered when demons and demonism are mentioned in their presence. Their Methodist sensibility, their practical good sense and cheerfulness, the Anglo-Saxon heritage of cozy realism and matter-of-factness make them suspicious of the unfamiliar, and resentful at the inexplicable.[6]

But for Margaret Atwood, human culture has always contained materialistic and instrumental values. They are the values of primitive man, "early / as caves and burned hair" ("Trainride: Vienna-Bonn"), of Odysseus ("Circe / Mud Poems"), of the gorgon's would-be 'lovers' in Double Persephone. Far from affirming history and time, as Jaspers argues, such commitment to instrumentality for Atwood constitutes an attempt to deny time by attempting Jaspers' "perfectionment of civilization." This is the import of the three Orpheus and Eurydice poems in Interlunar. Like many of the characters of Atwood's short fiction, Eurydice in the underworld has "grown used to silence"; Orpheus, in contrast, by his singing is involved in the instrumental use of language – to make Eurydice "become: living again."

I was your hallucination, listening
and floral, and you were singing me:
already new skin was forming on me
....
            ... already
there was dirt on my hands and I was thirsty.
("Orpheus (1)," I 59)

He attempts to sing Eurydice out of the underworld of transcendent being and into materiality. As the narrator of "Eurydice" remarks,

He wants you to be what he calls real.
He wants you to stop light.
He wants to feel himself thickening
like a treetrunk or a haunch ....

The phallic imagery of these lines, reminiscent of the "hook" "eye" image of *Power Politics,* signals his attachment to materiality – to the male role of space-filling or space-defining, and opposes the absence of "emptiness and silence" which characterizes Eurydice. Even his 'love' is defined by the material:

This love of his is not something
he can do if you aren't there,

in contrast to that of Eurydice who can "love him anywhere / even in this land of no memory." In Atwood's version of his story, he fails to win back Eurydice simply because of his empiricism; forbidden to look back at her, he turns to look anyway: "He cannot believe without seeing" ("Eurydice," *I* 61). In the much less satisfactory "Orpheus (2)" Atwood follows Orpheus to the moment when the women of the Ciconcs, jealous of his fixation on the lost Eurydice, tear him apart in "furious refusal". Even in death, however, he persists in his commitment to a quantifiable world –

Yet he will go on singing and in praise.
To sing is either praise
or defiance. Praise is defiance. (*I* 78)

– despite the fact that the women whom he by praising defies have demonstrably refused his defining song.

Visible throughout these three poems, as in most of Atwood's poems on mythological or documentary subjects, is a dehistoricizing of voice and detail. She makes no attempt to suggest the voice of a first-millenium B.C. Greek woman, or to evoke a precise historical setting. The setting is vague, "blanched dim corridors" (*I* 60), a "green light" (*I* 58). This imprecision has the effect simultaneously of denying the progressive theory of history described by Jaspers and of generalizing the experience of Orpheus and Eurydice, making it the experience of all humanity. Eurydice's cave thus becomes the encompassing vaginal world available to all women, and Orpheus's song, his "thickening flesh," the instrumentality grasped throughout history by most men. Such generalizing is, curiously, a rationalist technique which transforms Orpheus and Eurydice from individuals conditioned by experience and history into heraldic signs of a social ideology. This paradoxical use of a rationalist technique to achieve an anti-rationalist end is much more visible in Atwood's novels and criticism in which generalized literary patterns play major roles.

# CHAPTER THREE

# The Insufficiency of Poetry

---

this hope, this mouth-
ful of dirt, this poetry.
(*TS* 93)

UNDERLYING all of Margaret Atwood's poetry is a suggestion that the traditional artistic act, including the act of poetry, is a male use of space. Poetry may be the "carven word" of *Double Persephone,* a circle game, or the organized "square of paper" or the camera man.

Orange in the middle of a table:

It isn't enough
to walk around it
at a distance, saying
it's an orange:
("Against Still Life," *CG* 65)

Closely related to this concern is a decidedly formal or sculptural quality in the verse itself, a quality which led Robin Skelton to call her poems "timeless constructions."[1] In *Double Persephone* the static qualities of the piper's garden are reiterated in the pastoral diction and traditional stanza forms of the writing.

The shepherdess with giddy glance
Makes the amorous shepherd dance.
While sheep hurtle the stiles for love
And clouds pile featherbeds above.
("Pastoral," *DP* [5])

In *The Circle Game,* despite a move from literary to colloquial diction, the "word / plays, calculated ploys / of the body" which the persona decries are echoed in the detached, factual, and unemotional tone in which the persona speaks. Her verbs are often ones of static condition, her concerns are frequently spatial, where she is and, in this instance, of what size.

I am in the lake, in the centre
of the picture, just under the surface.

It is difficult to say where
precisely, or to say
how large or small I am.
("This is a Photograph of Me," CG 11)

At times in *The Circle Game,* this sense of detachment from self or from humankind in general is so complete that people are present only by synecdoche:

The small carved
animal is passed from
hand to hand
around the circle
until the stone grows warm

touching, the hands do not know
the form of animal
which was made or
the true form of stone
uncovered
("Carved Animals," CG 62)

Here, through both the synecdoche of "hands" and the passive voice of the opening verb the 'male' sculptural reality of the carved animal is made dominant. The syntax of the poem, which alternates "hands" and terms for the "carved animal" ("stone," "animal") in the subject position, further dehumanizes the "hands" by making them appear parallel if not equivalent to the carving. The language itself has a certain sculptural quality: the diction is factual, the rhythm dispassionate. By creating linguistically unlikely junctures which run counter to natural speech-pauses, the line-breaks imply an unmodulated and noncolloquial tone. The temporal dimension of language as an emotional and personal response to experience is thus largely eliminated.

This tendency to employ a 'male' spatial aesthetic is present in most of Atwood's early poetry especially in the poems overtly addressed to men. Here one often senses that the speaker has

purposely adopted the only language a male audience might understand – like an adult 'talking down' to a child. At the most elemen-
tary level, many of the central statements of the poems are assign-
ments of relative spatial position: "I walk across the bridge.... You
saunter beside me ..." (CG 12). "In the background there is a lake, /
and beyond that, some low hills ... / I am in the lake, ..." (CG 11).
"There is my country under glass, ... and beside it 10 blownup
snapshots ..." (AC 18). "When we were in it ... now / we are out of it
..." (PU 18). Adverbial phrases of location play key roles in many of
the poems: "kneeling on rock ... above me ... under my shadow" 7
(PU 8-9); "under a tree ... around you ... on the other side ... out of
sight" (PU 10); "in this garden ... outside the string borders ... in the
evening forest ... in the bay ... in another land" (PU 16-17); "Upon
the wall ... around it ... on the upper lip ... on the skin" (PU 46). Some
poems combine such phrases with statements of spatial position to
become entirely about relative spatial placement:

Beside this lake
....
my sister in bathing suit continues
her short desolate parade
to the end of the dock;

against the boards
her feet make sad statements
....

(I sit in a deckchair
....

She moves the raft out
....

            ... The sun encloses
rocks, trees, her feet in the water, the circling
bays and hills....

(Under my hand the paper
closes over these
marks ...

The words ripple ...
... towards the shore.)
("Younger Sister Going Swimming," PU 66-67)

Somewhat more revealing is the repeated concern of many of the poems with making statements of condition. The underlying implication of such statements is the existence of static qualities – identity, colour, shape: "This is before electricity ... the porch is wooden, / the house is wooden and grey ..."(PU 7); "She is / a raw voice ... She is everywhere, intrusive as the smells ... She is a bulk, a knot / swollen in space ... a raucous fact ... immutable" (AC 14-15). This concern with establishing the essence of things is further indicated by the large number of copula verbs in Atwood, especially in opening lines: "Here there are no armies" (PP 38); "You are / the lines I draw around you" (AC 60); "The streets are new" (JSM 50); "Marriage is not / a house" (PU 60); "There are two of them" (CG 68); "There are similarities" (CG). In Procedures for Underground and the subsequent collections of the 1970s most of the verbs are in the simple present tense and appear to indicate temporally uncircumscribed action.

The sun shines down

on two cars which have collided
at a turn-off, and rest
quietly on their sides

and on some cows which have come over,
nudge each other aside
at the fence, and stare.
("The End of the World," PU 32)

The static effect is amplified here and elsewhere by Atwood's selection of verbs denoting condition or minimal action – "Shines," "rest," "stare," "refuse," "permit," "become":

You refuse to own
yourself, you permit
others to do it for you:

you become slowly more public. (PP 30)

The temporal indeterminacy of such verbs can contribute to the creation of mythological or surrealistic effects:

I keep my parents in a garden
among lumpy trees, green sponges

on popsicle sticks. I give them a lopsided
sun which drops its heat
in spokes the colour of yellow crayon.

They have thick elephant legs,
....

("Eden is a Zoo," *PU* 6)

On other occasions this indeterminacy suggests habitual on-going
action and psychological estrangement from historical time:

I walk the cell, open the window,
shut the window, the little
motors click
and whir, I turn on all the
taps and switches

I take pills, I drink water, I kneel. (*PP* 19)

   The result of such techniques is the removal of time as an operative dimension from much of the poetry. The speaker appears to be a
spectator of her own life, standing outside both this life and its temporal context. The principle of cause and effect tends to disappear
under such circumstances; events become juxtaposed in space rather
than consecutively related. Such a condition prevails in "Progressive
Insanities of a Pioneer" where the natural 'oceanic' action of the land
is in no sense caused or precipitated by the pioneer who has juxtaposed himself to it. It prevails in "After the Flood, We" in which the
two lovers are introduced syntactically as parallel subjects – "I walk
across the bridge ... you saunter beside me" – inhabiting parallel but
self-contained experiences.

I walk across the bridge
towards the safety of high ground
....

gathering the sunken
bones of the drowned mothers
....

You saunter beside me, talking
of the beauty of the morning,
not even knowing
there's been a flood. (*CG* 12)

The syntactic parallelism is both ironic, in implying the existence of a relationship that is etiologically non-existent, and real, in specifying juxtaposition in space as the only operative link between its terms. A similar lack of cause and effect prevails between the lovers of *Power Politics* whose relationship, despite their physical interaction, also appears to be one of spatial juxtaposition rather than of mutual interaction.

You are the sun
in reverse, all energy
flows into you and is
abolished, you refuse
houses, ...

I lie mutilated beside
you; beneath us there are
sirens, fires ...

Here "you" and "I" are assigned parallel syntactic positions by the parallel syntax of "You are the sun" and "I lie ... beside you" The spatial quality of the relationship is underlined by "beside" and "beneath"; the latter preposition joins the lovers to a list ("sirens," "fires") of spatially related objects. This use of parallel syntax to indicate parallel but noninterlocking relationship is one of the principal technical resources of *Power Politics*.

You say: my other wives
are in there, they are all
beautiful and happy....

I say: it is only
a cupboard, my collection
of envelopes, ...

In your pockets the thin women
hang on their hooks ...

Around my neck I wear
the head of the beloved,.... (50)

In this instance the distinctness of the lovers is emphasized by the ironic contrast between the parallel syntax and nonparallel content. The woman's dialogue is a non sequitur to the man's; the items "around my neck" are similarly irrelevant to the items "in your pockets." No temporal or causal relationship exists within either pair of items. The links are spatial: the juxtaposed lovers, their syntactically juxtaposed pronouns, their syntactically juxtaposed "pockets" and "neck," and the general impression of juxtaposition created by the stanza arrangement. The overall effect is one of collage – collaged lovers, objects, and stanzas.

*

Clearly one question a reader must constantly ask when reading these poems is what signal is the tone of detachment meant to convey? If the speaker stands apart from what she describes, and even apart from her own role in it, where does she stand? In most cases it is the male spatially oriented world she stands apart from, the world of the pioneer or those "tourists of another kind" of "Totems." Where she writes from is a more difficult question. The content of the poems tells us she should write from "underground," from the living protean world of biological process that sends forth the nameless weeds and blizzards that bedevil those who would play circle games with time and space. But the language suggests otherwise; it is not protean, not 'liquid,' not a nameless bird or weed. It is more the language of someone in but not of the male formal garden, of someone physically within the arena of 'power politics' but refusing to seriously participate, of someone who has adopted 'male' language structures in order to communicate with men but who refuses to endorse such structures.

Often in the poems there is the implication that language itself may be male, may be one of the shovels or guns or circle games by which men attempt to re-shape process, and that the speaker must paradoxically enter the male spatial world to have any voice at all. The woman must use a man's own language to have any hope of being understood by him, his language of specified location and static condition, because he is uncomprehending of the underground or liquid. Otherwise she merely enrages the man, becomes one of the 'silent ones' whom men

... have assaulted daily, with shovels, axes, electric saws, the silent ones they accused of being silent because they would not speak in the received language.
("Circe / Mud Poems," *YAH* 49)

From a male point-of-view the female world of process may be 'silent,' pre-articulate,

words here are as pointless
as calling in a vacant
wilderness
("Journey to the Interior," CG 58)

much as its works are 'nameless' and 'aphoristic.' However, there is also the contrasting idea in these poems that there may be a female version of language – "a word, like an unclenching flower" – and that the male world, fearing this possibility, attempts to control and systematize language to maintain male power. In "Spell for the Director of Protocol" Atwood writes,

You would like to keep me
from saying anything, you would prefer it
if when I opened my mouth
nothing came out
but a white comic-strip balloon
with a question mark; or a blank button. (PU 45)

*

In the above poem the woman was a 'spell' caster, a speaker of magic words. The woman is often a magician in Atwood's work, a transformer, a producer of metamorphoses, who because of her participation in 'liquid' space can paradoxically alter both space and time much more easily than can the men who wish such alterations.

... the real question is
whether or not I will make you immortal.

At the moment only I
can do it ... (PP 5)

Sometimes she uses this metamorphic ability for her own protection, as in "She Considers Evading Him":

I can change my-
self more easily
than I can change you

I could grow bark and
become a shrub

or switch back in time
to the woman image left
in cave rubble, the drowned
stomach bulbed with fertility
....

or (better) speed myself up,
disguise myself in the knuckles
and purple-veined veils of old ladies. (*PP* 4)

But most often Atwood focusses on how the woman's transforming power has given her a role to play among men who wish, as does
the man in *Power Politics,* to have themselves or their world
transformed. The woman is a kind of artist here, also a kind a camera, lifting objects out of time, making them 'immortal.' The role is
one she has no particular interest in; "I liked you better the way you
were," the woman remarks after 'immortalizing' her lover in *Power
Politics.* The prototype for this woman is the "girl with the gorgon
touch" of *Double Persephone,* a girl who discovers the world of male
flesh turn before her eyes to postured stone. She is a naive, unwilling
transformer, still in the process of discovering both her power and
the strange wish of men to be 'marbled' by it. The women of *Power
Politics* and "The Circle Game" have become more accustomed to
men who wish things "fixed, stuck / down on the outspread map"
(*CG* 40) and can unenthusiastically play the male game as the price
of male companionship.

A fourth major portrait of this woman is Circe of "Circe / Mud
Poems," who because of a male 'story' must live on a timeless island
and participate in plots and landscapes for which she is "not responsible." Her island has become for her a place of "ennuie"; despite her
reputation for performing storybook transformations, mythological
men have become tiresome and predictable.

Men with the heads of eagles
no longer interest me
or pig men, or those who fly
with the aid of wax or feathers

or those who take off their clothes
to reveal other clothes
or those with skins of blue leather.

Like the gorgon girl, she hopes for the living flesh of men who would
be a relief from the closed narrative structure of an inherited life.

> I search instead for the others,
> the ones left over,
> the ones who have escaped from these
> mythologies with barely their lives,
> they have real faces and hands,.... (47)

Atwood's Odysseus, on the other hand, despite his awareness that
transformation out of time would destroy his individual existence,
appears strongly attracted by the timeless condition Circe can offer.
Circe accuses him of being passive, acquiescent, of fulfilling previously written narratives.

> The trees bend in the wind, you eat, you rest
> you think of nothing, your mind, you say,
> is like your hands, vacant (*YAH* 50)

> There must be more for you to do
> than permit yourself to be shoved
> by the wind from coast
> to coast to coast ...
> ....
> Don't you get tired of killing
> those whose deaths have been predicted
> and are therefore dead already

> Don't you get tired of wanting
> to live forever? (51)

The central point of "Circe / Mud Poems" is that Circe comes
alive and enters (bringing a reluctant Odysseus with her) female
space. The mythological story of Odysseus, his 'odyssey,' is tran-
scended or deconstructed. Odysseus gives up his implicit preference
that Circe be "simple," that she continue as a gorgonesque statue, a
"woman constructed out of mud," one who "began at the neck and
ended at the knees and elbows": "Is this what you would like me to
be, this mud woman? Is this what I would like to be? It would be so
simple"(61).

The crucial moment in Odysseus's change occurs when Circe
accedes to his request that she tell him the future (and thereby act out
her role as magical woman).

Here are the holy birds,
grub white, with solid blood
wobbling on their heads and throats

Circe sardonically begins this conscious parody of the Roman custom of divining the future in a bird's entrails. Odysseus's "holy"
birds, symbolic of controlled or perfect space, "wobble" unexpect-
edly with the biological chaos of blood and grub. The act of prophecy results not in the order and predictability that Odysseus
wanted but in confusion – in female space rather than the expected
male. "As you can see," Circe tells him

The future is a mess,
snarled guts all over the yard. (66)

Beneath the macabre humour, both woman as priestess and religion
as a container for biology have been discredited. In the following section a further discrediting of Odysseus's inherited story occurs –
winter. "You didn't expect that / it isn't supposed to occur on this
kind of island," Circe teases him. The poem ends on yet one more
disruption: Circe now has two islands instead of one. As well as the
familiar one where "events run themselves through / almost without
us," where life "goes and goes, I could recite it backwards," is a new
unpredictable one which Circe knows "nothing about / because it
has never happened." This second is an autumnal island, not timeless
but subject to time and decay, where

the grass is yellow, tinged
with grey, the apples
are still on the trees,
... the wet [snow] flakes
falling onto our skin and melting.

And where presumably the lovers can proceed into a story that is,
like the stream on this island, "not frozen yet," that departs from all
others.

*

Is there poetry on this second island where Circe and Odysseus are
left, where Circe no longer fills her roles of magician and priestess? Is
there language and art, or are these only tools for making statues of

mud women and calculated histories such as those woven over and over by deserted Penelope until she gets one that Odysseus "will believe in"(65). Circe herself speaks directly only once of art, and disparagingly. In the course of one of her many warnings to Odysseus she remarks "So much for art. So much for prophecy." Elsewhere words in the poem are most often associated with the prison of the timeless – with the "ruthless" inherited story, with Penelope's arbitrary histories, with the life Circe can "recite backwards."

The poems of Atwood's 1981 collection, *True Stories*, a book which questions the reliability of *story* on numerous occasions ("the true story is vicious / and multiple and untrue"), contain a number of references to the limitations of language and poetry. In some of these, poetry is merely ineffectual, unequal to the task of speaking the horrors of ongoing reality, a mere

... distraction, takes your mind
off work or the jerky screen
where death is an event, love
isn't unless it's double
suicide. How can I justify
this gentle poem then in the face of sheer
horror. A genteel pretence, ...
("Small Poems for the Winter Solstice," *TS* 34)

Poetry here is either flawed,

This poem is mournful
and sentimental and filled
with complaints....

or else an impossible ideal, a "bouquet of nice clean words." The result is paradoxically a poem about no poem, with a 'wordless' speaker giving us words from the female realm of inarticulate liquids we see so often in Atwood.

That's me on the corner, sleet

down my neck, wordless. (*TS* 32)

In "Damside," another poem in *True Stories*, poetry is obliquely condemned as the opposite of life's time-bound reality: "If this were a poem you'd live forever." Again we seem confronted by a paradox

– what we had thought was a poem is not a poem; it is "only ... poor weather ... a prayer, a sewer, a prayer"(99).

In the major 'poem' of *True Stories*, "Notes towards a Poem which Can Never Be Written," poetry is once again unequal to the realities it must confront. The atrocities and indignities afflicted on men and women by political torturers in the name of political order leave "no poem you can write about it."

We make wreaths of adjectives for them,
we count them like beads
we turn them into statistics and litanies
and into poems like this one.

Nothing works.
They remain what they are.

We are given yet another paradox. What we have read is both one of "poems like this one" and of "Notes towards a Poem that Can Never Be Written." Atwood has used "poem" here in two senses, a female one in which the poem is protean, metamorphic, liquid, underground, and therefore simultaneously "true" and "never to be written" and a male one in which it is quantifying ("we count them like beads"), repetitive ("litanies") and inaccurate.

*

A note toward a poem which can never be written: to write such an unpoem is to deny the artificial poem, the "wreath of adjectives," the male 'circle game' which such a poem is part of, and ultimately to deny the male analytic and technological approach to reality that the conventional 'poet' and the torturer share. Here is the central line of continuity in Atwood's poetry: that the city planner of *The Circle Game*, the lovers who "touch as though attacking" (*PP* 37), the artist who writes an authoritative, analytic poem, and the torturer who regards the human body as an object to be manipulated, subdued, and dissected are engaged in aesthetically similar (though morally dissimilar) tasks. Atwood writes only "notes toward a poem" because to pretend to do otherwise would be to treat language and experience in the same way that the political technician treats a prisoner to create a "banner," an art, a "flag."

... the knife ... cuts loves
out of your flesh like tumours,

leaving you breastless
and without a name,
flattened, bloodless, even your voice
cauterized by too much pain,

a flayed body untangled
string by string and hung
to the wall, an agonized banner
displayed for the same reason
flags are.
("Torture," *TS* 51)

*

I make this charm
from nothing but paper; which is good
for exactly nothing.

If conventional poetry is indeed at best ineffectual, and at worst manipulative, distorting, and imprisoning, what sorts of writing are possible to a poet who would oppose 'the circle game'? Do Margaret Atwood's poems manage to be such poetry?

Real poetry in Atwood's vision is largely gestural, momentarily symbolic, non-linguistic. It is the work of the female left hand, not of the male right. It is not the word of the dying woman lying

on the wet cement floor
under the unending light
needle marks on her arms put there
to kill the brain.

Rather it is her body's shape and motion.

It is her body, silent
and fingerless, writing this poem.

The poem is a gesture of creativity amid the carnage left by male political logic – the work and song of a vulture feasting in the "territory of murder."

I make life, which is a prayer.
I make clean bones.
I make a grey zinc noise
which to me is a song.
("Vultures," *TS* 73)

It is biological – the digestion of death to produce life, or as in
"Mushrooms," the transformation of earth and leafmold into the
"nipples ... cool white fishgills, / leathery purple brains" of newly
born fungi. Often when Atwood speaks of such creation there is a
sense of giving birth, as here where the word "midsoil" suggests
'midwife' and the mushrooms themselves are humanized with brain,
hair, fingers, and "eyeblinks."

Underfoot there's a cloud of rootlets,
shed hairs or a bundle of loose threads
blown slowly through the midsoil.
These are their flowers, these fingers
reaching through darkness to the sky,
these eyeblinks
that burst and powder the air with spores.
...
they smell of death and the waxy
skins of the newborn,
flesh into earth into flesh. (TS 91-93)

But above all, these children are poems, as Atwood's last lines here
insist – "this hope, this mouth- / ful of dirt, this poetry." The clear
implication of the poem is that the poet is metaphorically female,
that the act of poetry is a giving birth, that the "mouth" of poetry is
not the male oracular head of bardic recitation or of Judaic prophecy
but the vagina and its wordless speakings. A similar sense of poetry is
given in "Spelling" where Atwood draws a parallel between the male
fear of the words of witches and male anger at woman's ability to
bear.

I return to the story
of the woman caught in the war
& in labour, her thighs tied
together by the enemy
so she could not give birth

Ancestress: the burning witch
her mouth covered by leather
to strangle words.

A word after a word
after a word is power (TS 63-64)

Although earlier in this poem Atwood has said "a child is not a poem, / a poem is not a child," the parallel Atwood draws makes childbirth, as she says later, "a metaphor" – a metaphor which underlines the femaleness of words, the femaleness of inspired speech.

\*

In the last stanza of "Spelling" Atwood announces a curious 'naming' to be done by the speaker's infant daughter who is "learning how to spell." It is curious because elsewhere in Atwood, as in "Progressive Insanities of a Pioneer," naming is an Adamic act, the male imposition of arbitrary order on the female garden. The suggestion in this stanza is that there is an alternate naming, and (just as there are two kinds of poetry) perhaps an alternate language, grounded in female "blood" as well as male "sky and sun."

How do you learn to spell?
Blood, sky and the sun,
your own name first,
your first naming, your first name,
your first word.

"Blood" here is notably the first word, the name that is "your own name first." This new naming, this alternate language, arguably rests on affirming first the biological reality – i.e. the individual woman's reality ("your first name") which incorporates the biological. What kind of language is this? The pun in the poem's title, "Spelling," suggests that it is double, perhaps simultaneously female and male, connotative and denotative, pre-rational and rational. In semiotic terms, it is a 'first-order language,' which rests on a direct connotative relationship between the word and its signified; the 'male' language it resists is in contrast a generalizing 'second-order' language which empties the signified of its history and particularity, making a woman's body into a "flag," a particular man into a "mythology." This male second-order language (which in Atwood's novels ultimately manifests itself as modish cliché phrases – "go with the flow" – which homogenize individual life) not only deprives individual words like "go" and "flow" of meaning but argues an ideology of conformity – "flag," "mythology" – which submerges individual experience.

*

There being two languages in Atwood, the female connotative and male denotative, and two poetries, the female 'gesture' symbolized by biological process and the male process-fixing "bouquet of nice clean words," one might look again at the ostensibly sculptural qualities of much of her poetry and at the "modular" and "timeless" structural principles Robin Skelton believes he can identify in it. Perhaps his modular stanzas are not stanzas at all in the conventional sense but, like the spontaneously growing wild plants of the pioneer's farm, are "aphorisms," "nameless weeds," gestures of poetic thought. Perhaps the discontinuity Skelton observed between them is a lack of that 'male' continuity which expects serial occurrences rather than concurrent ones, which expects single strands of narrative structure rather than multiple ones.

In many cases the seemingly discontinuous stanzas may be co-present, may be alternatives to each other rather than successors.

Destruction shines with such beauty

Light on his wet hair
serpents of blood jerked from the wrists

Sun thrown from the raised and lowered
rifles / debris of the still alive

Your left eye, green and lethal
("Newsreel: Man and Firing Squad," YAH 8)

At times Atwood declares such a disjunctive relationship.

Alternate version: you advance
through the grey streets of this house, ... (PP 49)

or you will descend through the roof
with the spurious authority of a
government official,
....
or you will be slipped under
the door, your skin furred with cancelled
airmail stamps,.... (PP 30)

The ordering of a disjunctively structured poem is not 'timeless' but part of an alternative system of time. Male time is measured time; its

alternative is not static but fluid, metamorphic, multiple, without
temporal landmarks, in motion but not systematically in motion.
Atwood poems characteristically change moods and directions
between stanzas, change syntax, occasionally change points of view.
Such poems are not atemporal in being outside of process, only in
being outside rationalized time.

*

The ruinous huts, the parts
of children gnawed by cats, the cooking
fires left smouldering, the cairns
of bones arranged so neatly.
In the service
of the word.
("A Massacre Before It Is Heard About," *I* 73)

Certainly Margaret Atwood has created a difficult theoretical framework within which to write. If conventional language is a second-
order language, rational, analytic, and male, and its alternative is
aphoristic, 'wordless,' and gestural, then Atwood's choices are only
to give up conventional language altogether, perhaps in favour of a
kind of mime or one of the plastic arts, or to work subversively in the
alien medium to combine it with her own. She has chosen the second,
writing words which paradoxically affirm the silent and wordless.
The theme of escape from rationalized time and articulated space
into unmeasured pre-articulate process is a constant in Atwood's
work. From the gorgon-girl of *Double Persephone* who yearns to
abandon literary space for the uncertainties of biology, to the
speaker of *True Stories* who celebrates the birth of mushrooms as a
moment of 'poetry,' Atwood concerns herself with the tyranny of
conventional language, of inherited story, of cultural and sexual
stereotype, and with the contrasting richness of 'female' kinetic reality. Unfortunately, art for Atwood always has the male "gorgon
touch," working to transform process into structure, disorder into
order, flesh into stone. All of her female artist-figures, the girl of
*Double Persephone,* the Power Politician who transforms her lover
into a comic book hero, Susanna Moodie who can remake her husband into "her idea of him" (*JSM* 19), Circe who can "create,
manufacture" hierarchic lovers *YAH* 47) have this masculine artistic
power, and can dispassionately use it to survive in a patriarchal

culture. The struggle of the women to abandon art, and affirm natural process, is amplified by Atwood's own mixed feelings about the art of language into the writer's personal struggle. In its double-ness, this struggle can be resolved only through irresolution, only through endless paradox and oxymoron. It repeats itself throughout Atwood's writing in different dramatic contexts – the North Ameri-can wilderness, contemporary marriage, Latin-American political violence. In each book, Atwood's language communicates to the reader the presence of a consciousness both detached from the con-ventional language-system it is using and (by virtue of its using this language-system) at some distance from the 'wordless' female realm it prefers. The reader thus experiences vicariously the dissociations from natural process which imprisonment in the circle game creates. The power of the poems is expanded by the implicit information in their language and form that the consciousness behind them suffers the same dissociations and alienations that the poems decry. Like Circe and Medusa, this consciousness has artistic flux-ordering powers which it dislikes using, has insight into process which only its alienation from process allows it to express in visible words. Like a mirror, it creates art at the expense of its own participation in pro-tean reality, at the expense of its "breath," "anger," and "joy."

Don't assume it is passive
or easy, this clarity

with which I give you yourself.
Consider what restraint it

takes: breath withheld, no anger
or joy disturbing the surface

of the ice.
You are suspended in me

beautiful and frozen, I
preserve you, in me you are safe.

It is not a trick either,
it is a craft

mirrors are crafty.
("Tricks with Mirrors," YAH 26)

As Eli Mandel has written, Atwood seems to have involved herself in "an impossible dilemma about writing and experience, or about fiction and wisdom."[2] Male order may constitute a travesty of female chaos and its gestural language, but only a wary appropriation of that order enables a speaking of either.

# CHAPTER FOUR

# Four Female 'Comedies'

---

Everything from history must be eliminated,
the circles and the arrogant square pages. (S 176)

IN VIEW of the argument of Atwood's poetry that *pattern* is a
humanistic 'male' second-order imposition on experience, it is curious that four of Atwood's five novels appear to be written in a traditional narrative pattern. The apparent pattern is that of comedy,
which begins in social disruption, sends its characters into a healing
'green world,' and returns them to society capable of restoring it to
wholeness – this new capability often being symbolized by a marriage or a birth. Atwood's characters, however, face a slightly different task of healing from that of traditional comedy. Their task is
more to heal themselves than to heal society. In this healing they
must not only deliver themselves from the damage done to them by
the male concepts of order and language we have seen in the poetry,
but also attempt in some way to deliver themselves from the inherited patriarchal narrative pattern in which Atwood has located them
– i.e. from the comic pattern itself. Only one of the four central characters comes close to achieving both.

*

All four novels present us with a young woman of some sensitivity
who has found herself isolated among form-asserting and technologically inclined people. All four protagonists attempt to escape, those
of *The Edible Woman* and *Surfacing* through unconscious rebellion,
those of *Lady Oracle* and *Bodily Harm* by flight to another country.
Each woman appears to have an unconscious perception of the
threat which her present situation constitutes to her integrity well
before her mind gains a corresponding insight. In the first two novels,
the protagonists' bodies both attempt leadership of the whole
woman in order to bring her to knowledge and safety. They attempt
to flee, they refuse food, they prohibit certain actions. A kind of

madness seizes the woman, a madness in which her new pre-conscious and body-dominated perspective makes everyday events seem frighteningly surrealistic. Her images of the world become prelogical, 'underground,' discontinuous, yet deliver convincing symbolic truth. In *The Edible Woman*, the protagonist's fiancé – who is characterized by the same camera and weapons imagery of male rationalism that is found in Atwood's poetry – attempts to photograph her:

That dark intent marksman with his aiming eye had been there all the time, hidden by the other layers, waiting for her at the dead centre: a homicidal maniac with a lethal weapon in his hands. (*EW* 246 )

In *Surfacing* a group of friends and acquaintances attempt to 'rescue' her from apparent insanity and return her to 'normal' city life:

They're hulking out of the boat now, four or five of them. I can't see them clearly, their faces, the stems and leaves are in the way, but I can smell them and the scent brings nausea, it's stale air, bus stations, and nicotine smoke, mouths lined with soiled plush, acid taste of copper wiring or money. Their skins are red, green in squares, blue in lines, and it's a minute before I remember that these are fake skins, flags. (*S* 183-184)

These friends are also characterized by Atwood's male imagery of technology and analytic division – "red, green in squares." In both cases the onset of madness results in the narrative viewpoint changing from first to third person. In both, when the protagonist achieves some conscious insight into the male danger she has escaped from, her body can surrender its control of her to a somewhat reintegrated person. At the moment of insight each comes to view her problem symbolically as having her "neck ... closed over, ... shutting me into my head ..." (*S* 121).

In *Lady Oracle* and *Bodily Harm* two more women are sufficiently detached and alienated to experience their friends and relatives as utter strangers. One, overwhelmed by plots and dangers she imagines around her, escapes not into madness but into a mad act of pretended suicide and improvised exile. The other less dramatically escapes superficial friendships ("most of her friends were really just contacts" [*BH* 16]), superficial sex ("a pleasant form of communication, like gossip" [*BH* 102]), an ominously perceived lover ("white teeth and narrow muzzle grinning like a fox" [*BH* 103]) and the surprise of a partial mastectomy to vacation on a remote

Caribbean island. In 'exile' both women achieve a new vision of their own lives and of the violence latent in the various men they have known; at the end of the novels both women feel prepared – naively in Joan Foster's case – to lead more realistic and self-fulfilling lives on their return home.

*

The structural similarities between the books are impressive – alienation from natural process, followed by descent into a more primitive but healing reality, and finally some return to personal wholeness through renewed recognition of natural force. In bare outline, Atwood's comic structure resembles the Shakespearean sequence of social disorder, exile into a healing 'green world,' reintegration to society and return to natural order. The parallel, however, points to significant differences. Atwood's concern is with process much more than with 'order'; order for her is a male word used by 'packagers' like Rennie's lover Jake who decides "how things would look and ... what people would feel about them" (*BH* 103). Her immediate goal is not to change society but to change the individual woman – often minimally – to survive with some integrity in that society. Her green world, the Shakespearean source of healing power, is the personal unconscious: Marian MacAlpin's paralyzing fear of eating, the delusion of the protagonist of *Surfacing* that she is a part of the victimized wilderness, Joan Foster's fantasies that she lives in Costume Gothic romance, Rennie Wilford's prison vision of the archetypal "man with a rope" that lurks behind the plastic face of each technological man.

Atwood's denouements leave her protagonists – somewhat like Shakespeare's Miranda – in a deeply flawed male world about which they still hold some illusions. *Lady Oracle*'s Joan Foster, who in her excessive sentimentality is a parody of Miranda, is about to repeat her habitual behaviour pattern of absurd trust followed by absurd distrust with yet another man. Her illusions go far beyond those of Miranda in that they fantasize evil as much as they do the brave and new. Her story is her discovery of how her projections of Gothic malevolence and glamour onto everyday reality have prevented her from seeing the actual rewards and dangers of the everyday. She finds she has prevented herself from experiencing those around her as real people – has, for example, transformed her tweedy husband Arthur into a Brontëan hero – and from recognizing the real threats which some of them, usually through their own fantasies, constitute to her. The Gothic plot formula, a staple of the publisher for whom she pseudonymously writes pulp fiction, is clearly an inherited male structure from which Joan must escape, yet at the end of the novel, as she impulsively changes her view of the reporter she has assaulted from 'hired killer' to 'helpless young man,' she seems ready to discard her various discoveries and re-enter the Gothic script. The killer / nice young man dichotomy is the basic distortion in both the Gothic formula and Joan's image of the world; she has seen her father as both a murderer and a healing doctor, the "daffodil man" who lurked in her childhood ravine as both a molester and a rescuer, her husband as both "furtive" (104) and idealistic (165). Her failures to integrate these extreme visions reflects finally a failure to integrate the underground and surface elements (Atwood might say female and male elements) in her personality.

A character closer to Shakespeare's Miranda is Marian MacAlpin of *The Edible Woman*. She is the youngest of Atwood's comic protagonists, the ingenue who may yet grow out of her limitations through experience. She cheerfully enters the male world of corporate law, bathtub sex, plastic apartment blocks, and market research – the world of "Moose Beer" – not because she believes in it but because she has never questioned it. Her story is her discovery not of her own fantasies but of the violent male fantasies which surround her in her job as a market researcher and in her impending marriage to a young lawyer. Although younger, she is at a stage of awareness beyond that of Joan Foster.

Both Rennie Wilford of *Bodily Harm* and the unnamed narrator of *Surfacing* are yet a stage further. The latter is a cynic who has come to accept brutality, superficiality, and the will to power as "normal" aspects of the human condition, and who has learned to protect herself through a kind of mechanical detachment and efficiency of her own. Her story is her discovery that she contains the predatory and technological within herself; that her male twin (symbolically represented by her brother) has repeatedly expressed itself in her 'adjustive' coping with the male world. Rennie Wilford is a similar character, who has also learned how to repress unconscious need beneath a superficially expressed pattern of social convention. She too works in the Toronto media community, a "lifestyle" journalist rather than a book illustrator. Her story is her discovery of human love and compassion, a discovery that beyond the unthinking madness of mechanical action – the cliché 'openness' of her Toronto friends' mottoes, "go with the flow," "keep your options open" – profound emotions are still possible.

*

... I can feel my lost child surfacing within me, forgiving me, rising from the lake where it has been prisoned for so long, its eyes and teeth phosphorescent, the two halves clasp, interlocking like fingers....

Much of the recent critical interpretation of Atwood's fiction has argued that Atwood uses the comic narrative pattern or its cognate, the pattern of quest romance, to express feminine consciousness. Comedy's retreat to the green world or romance's descent into disorientation and horror are read as doorways into 'new places' of feminine essence from which an Atwood protagonist may return with increased confidence in her womanhood. "Marian [MacAlpin] is, in a sense, the romantic hero / heroine who searches for her identity through a quest which takes her on a dark voyage into the underworld and back," writes Catherine McLay.[1] Annis Pratt offers a reading of *Surfacing* in which the novel becomes a model of "woman's rebirth fiction" in which "the hero plunges down through subconscious to unconscious materials and is empowered by absorbing the archetypal symbols available to her."[2] With somewhat less rhetoric but equivalent optimism, Barbara Rigney places *Surfacing* in a tradition of "alienated female consciousness" and writes

> Thus the protagonist, like Lessing's Martha, loses a tenuous identity only to regain a firmer one. She surfaces from the illogical to return to a world of logic, but not now, as before, divided, incapable of coping.... To the protagonist belongs the ultimate sanity: the knowledge that woman can descend, and return, sane, whole, victorious.[3]

Disappointingly, none of these commentators recognize that the comic or romance patterns are themselves patriarchal second-order constructions from which, to be 'free' in any meaningful way, Atwood characters will have to escape. It is not so much that these patterns have been articulated by men or shaped over the centuries by a male-dominated culture, as that they are patterns, formulas, and thus inherently 'male' within the solid versus liquid, fenced versus unfenced, male-female definitions Atwood develops throughout her work. As most graphically shown in *Lady Oracle*, where all of Joan

Bennett's reflections on herself are sabotaged by the formulae of Gothic romance, the patterns confine rather than liberate, they assign the woman to a narrative structure rather than allow her to find a narrative authentic to herself.

In the terms of Atwood's vision of male and female, critics such as McLay, Rigney, and Pratt appear to have chosen the male 'rationalist' role – not only by their using the 'surface' language of discursive prose but by their adopting, without irony, schematic critical approaches. Pratt's article emulates the analytic method of the research scientist, proceeding from hypothesis to summary through paragraphs entitled "Phase I," "Phase II," "Phase III," "Phase IV," etc., and implies throughout the "calculated ploys," maps, and "cold blue thumbtacks" of the man of "The Circle Game" rather than any female liberation. Rigney methodically ties *Surfacing* to novels by Brontë, Woolf, and Lessing, and to the psychiatric model of R.D. Laing's *The Divided Self*, in her search for "role models for the psychological growth of women." The very notion of a "role model" in Atwood's vision is male. Catherine McLay reduces *The Edible Woman* to plot summary in her attempt to illustrate a step by step reiteration of the archetypal Romance.

*

I'm what they call a commercial artist.... For a while I was going to be a real artist; he [her art teacher and lover] thought that was cute but misguided, he said I should study something I'd be able to use because there have never been any important woman artists ... and so I went into Design and did fabric patterns. (*S* 52)

The careers of Atwood's comic heroines make an interesting commentary not only on the 'design and pattern' critics above but on the role of pattern in the novels themselves. All four protagonists are artists of some kind – three are writers and one a visual artist. All four shape their art to meet the required patterns of male employers; Marian does book illustrations for "Mr. Perceval the publisher ... a cautious man," who "shies away from anything he calls 'disturbing.'"

So I compromised; now I compromise before I take the work in, it saves time. I've learned the sort of thing he wants: elegant and stylized, decoratively coloured, like patisserie cakes. I can do that, I can imitate anything, fake Walt Disney, Victorian etchings in sepia, Bavarian cookies, ersatz Eskimo for the home market. (*S* 53)

Marian MacAlpin's job at Seymour Surveys is to write "useful" prose, to revise the company's "questionnaires, turning the convoluted and overly-subtle prose of the psychologists who write them into simple questions which can be understood by the people who ask them as well as the people who answer them. A question like 'In what percentile would you place the visual impact value?' is not useful" (*EW* 19). Her shaping of words to meet the needs of others parallels her shaping of herself to please Peter, as when she turns herself into a work of sculpture to dress for his party.

She held both of her naked arms out towards the mirror. They were the only portion of her flesh that was without a cloth or nylon or leather or varnish covering, but in the glass even they looked fake, like soft pinkish-white rubber or plastic, boneless, flexible.... (*EW* 229)

The feeling that she is leading a synthetic life, one artificially created to match patterns set by others, pervades the consciousness of Rennie in *Bodily Harm*. In her journalism she consciously tailors her words to suit a market; when writing for women's magazine using

the assumption ... that ... the source of the powerful ergs of boredom, was male, and that the passive recipient was female. Of course this was unfair, but who except women would read a *Pandora* 'Relationships' column? When writing for male-oriented magazines such as *Crusoe* or *Visor* she offered self-help hints: 'How to Read Her Mind.' (19)

Correspondingly, she feels her life echoing the clichés of her journalism, sees herself becoming a statistic in an article on cancer, taking a Caribbean holiday for "Fun in the Sun" (16), thinking of her doctor as a hypothetical article "When Doctors Get Sick" (85).

All of these women feel trapped by the static patterns of their art and attempt in some way to challenge or destroy these patterns. Rennie becomes increasingly aware of the ironic disparity between her journalistic catchwords and the actual events she encounters – how the words "seven jewel-like beaches" are made to denote something "narrow and gravelly and dotted with lumps of coagulated oil"(79). By baking her woman-shaped cake, Marian finally parodies Peter's expectation that she will become a female mannequin. The narrator of *Surfacing* takes a more direct approach, destroying her derivative childhood drawings, slashing the clothes that have become, like Marian's, "fake" and "plastic."

As a writer of Costume Gothic fiction, Joan Foster encompasses the derivativeness of all these characters. Like Rennie, she employs a prescribed vocabulary, "I made lists of words like 'fichu' and 'paletot' and 'pelisse'; I spent whole afternoons in the costume room of the Victoria and Albert Museum," she tells us. Like Marian, she learns that appropriate clothing can contrive almost any effect; "I thought if I could only get the clothes right, everything else would fall into line. And it did...." Like the narrator of *Surfacing,* she models her art to meet the requirements of others; "My first effort came back with instructions. I made the necessary revisions and received my first hundred pounds"(156). Worse, she follows all three characters in shaping the 'plot' of her own life on the basis of received pattern – for her the narrative conventions of her novels. Her relationships with men are repeatedly falsified by her delusion that a love affair inevitably obeys the 'flight from demon lover' motif of her "Stalked by Love," "Escape from Love," and "Love, My Ransom." In all four Atwood novels pattern enslaves and limits the protagonists; it sterilizes their art and prevents fulfilling relationships with others.

*

"I have to recant, give up the old belief that I'm powerless," *Surfacing*'s narrator tells herself on its final page. All four of Atwood's protagonists display extreme passivity, often believing their lives to be determined by narratives entirely outside their control. Marian MacAlpin believes she is fated to marry, suspects that she may be at the mercy of unconscious forces that are pushing her to marry Peter, for whom she actually cares very little.

Of course I'd always assumed through highschool and college that I was going to marry someone eventually and have children, everyone does. Either two or four,.... But although I'm sure it was in the back of my mind, I hadn't consciously expected it to happen so soon or quite the way it did. Of course I was more involved with Peter all along than I wanted to admit. (*EW* 102)

In *Surfacing* the protagonist feels that "there's no act I can perform except waiting," that it would be fruitless to try to change her "compromise" career as a commercial artist or to try to alter her unsatisfactory relationship with Joe. In *Bodily Harm* Rennie Wilford wishes to appear ordinary; "she aims for neutrality; she needs it for her work, as she used to tell Jake. Invisibility"(15). She has repudiated her hopes to be an "honest" journalist,

Once she had ambitions, which she now thinks of as illusions: she believed there was a right man, not several and not almost right, and she believed there was a real story, not several and not almost real.

*Lady Oracle* brings such passivity into clear focus. Joan Foster drifts from job to job, relationship to relationship. She sees little in life that she could be passionately attached to. She becomes Paul's mistress because "if you find yourself in a situation you can't get out of gracefully, you might as well pretend you chose it"(149). She meets her future husband by "accident" (134), and consents to marry him because she "couldn't think of any reasons why not"(197).

*

I'd allowed myself to be cut in two. Woman sawn apart in a wooden crate, wearing a bathing suit, done with mirrors, I read it in a comic book, only with me there had been an accident and I came apart. The other half, the one locked away, was the only one that could live; I was the wrong half, detached, terminal. I was nothing but a head, or no, something minor like a severed thumb; numb. (S 124-125)

There is so much Gothic imagery – of dismemberment, imprisonment, trick mirrors, dungeons, mazes, disembowelings – in these four novels that at times it is difficult to remember that it is the contemporary family rather than Gothic romance which is their primary focus. In some ways – as the failure of Rigney's and McLay's criticism suggests – the Gothic element is a red herring, because for Atwood's protagonists it constitutes an escape from reality rather than a reality in its own right. At worst, it is a projection they have placed on reality, a lie they have told about it, a logical pattern they have imposed upon it. At best, as above, the Gothic is a metaphor that will help them understand reality, but which they cannot allow to replace it.

All four comic protagonists are liars. They tell lies in their professional work, they lie and fantasize as narrators of the novels, they fictionalize – on derivative models – their own lives to themselves. The most blatant fictionalizer of her own life is Joan Bennett, whose Costume Gothics are overt simplifications of her own love affairs. These novels exaggerate goodness and villainy, exaggerate the similarities between goodness and villainy; ultimately these exaggerations expose – even for Joan – the fraudulence of her dual views of people like her husband (assassin and knight errant) and her father (hired killer and healer). She has fictionalized not only a false interpretation of her own life ("Lady Oracle") but three distinct personal identities – as Joan Delacourt, conventionally thin child, Louisa K. Delacourt, author of Gothic fiction, and Joan Foster, author of *Lady Oracle*. Her favourite fictional framework for reinterpreting her life is the romance of maiden-in-flight – from obesity (as Joan Delacourt), from an enchanted prison (as Lady Oracle or Tennyson's Lady of Shalott), or from the attractive rapacious man (as Joan Bennett or Charlotte / Felicia of the Costume Gothics). The failure of the Gothic framework to support Joan's life discredits the Gothic as a solution to a woman's difficulties, even as Atwood's novel, by using the framework, appears to confirm it.

The fictions constructed by the narrators of the other three novels are somewhat less visible but no less significant. At the heart of *Surfacing* is the life the narrator has invented about having been married, given birth, and been divorced. Accompanying it are various Gothic fictions – that her brother had once drowned, that the married teacher who had once got her pregnant was both a 'saint' and a murderer, that the nearby villagers will "shoot" or "bludgeon" her(212). Pervading all these is the fiction of the life-role she had invented for herself back in city – "calm ... cool ... as if I were feeling no emotion"(28). At the beginning of *The Edible Woman* is the script Marian had adopted in which she could play sensible "stolid" woman; at the end is the pretended self of the cake-doll which she bakes and consumes, in the middle yet another derivative fiction in which her fiancé Peter plays cynical hunter and herself his helpless prey. While all these fictions contain symbolic and metaphoric truth – Peter is oppressive, the villagers in *Surfacing* indeed will not understand the narrator's nakedness – they also distort the very facts they only partly illuminate. Only when *Surfacing*'s narrator can discard her fictions about her married lover can she see that "He was neither of the things I believed, he was only a normal man, middle-aged, second-rate, selfish and kind in the average proportions, ..." (189).

In *Bodily Harm* Rennie consistently must resist the temptation to fictionalize reality. When she is diagnosed as having cancer, she thinks immediately "she could do a piece on it. 'Cancer, the Coming Thing.' *Homemaker's* might take it, or *Chatelaine*. How about 'The Cutoff Point'"(27). In her shoddy Caribbean hotel room she begins composing "The decor is nondescript, resembling nothing so much as an English provincial hotel, with flowered wallpaper ..." (42). The novel concludes with two rescue fantasies (identifiable by their future tense) which Rennie composes amid the increasing horror of a political prison.

The fascination of the protagonists of *The Edible Woman, Surfacing* and *Lady Oracle* with both the Gothic image and an archetypal interpretation of their own lives as Gothic romance, as helpless maiden besieged by lecherous landlord (who may, as in Samuel Richardson's archetypal *Pamela,* be potentially the rescuing and virtuous prince), understandably invites archetypal interpretations of the novels themselves. Thus McLay's "*The Edible Woman* as Romance," Pratt's "*Surfacing* as the Rebirth Journey," Rigby's "Descent and Return in *Surfacing.*" Such interpretations, however, confuse the characters' fictions with the author's fiction, mistake novels which deconstruct archetypes for novels which confirm them. Ultimately they mistake Freudian novels, which root personal liberation in a cathartic acknowledgement of the subconscious, for Jungian ones.

*

Rennie's mother comes in through the kitchen door, carrying a brown paper bag full of groceries. She has on one of her shopping dresses, navy blue.

What's going on? she says to Rennie. I can't find my hands, says her grandmother.

Rennie's mother looks with patience and disgust at Rennie, at her grandmother, at the kitchen and the peanut butter sandwich and the groceries she's carrying. She sets the bag down carefully on the table. Don't you know what to do by now? she says to Rennie. Here they are. Right where you put them. She takes hold of the grandmother's dangling hands, clasping them in her own. (*BH* 297-298)

Throughout the four novels the role of family relationships, particularly that between mother and daughter, increases in importance. As it does it correspondingly increases the psychological depth of the books and the credibility of the narrator's emotions and actions. In *The Edible Woman,* where the narrator's childhood and adolescence (and with them her relationship with her parents) are unmentioned, the psychological perspective is shallow. We are given no understanding of the source of Marian's fears, projections, and transferences. From what childhood dramas do the feelings come that cause her to see her employer as a heartless parent, her fiancé Peter as a predator, his apartment building as a steel and plastic monster? What has attracted her to "nicely packaged" Peter, or to Ainsley, her self-important roommate? Marian's own explanation that these seemed like practical or conventional choices only begs the larger question of why practicality should be important to her, or why she should have so little passion as to believe herself satisfied with the practical and convenient.

It would be possible to argue that such psychological considerations are irrelevant to *The Edible Woman* were it not for the fact that in three subsequent novels, which involve similar situations and narrators, Atwood makes family relations a central element. *Surfacing* begins with views of the protagonist's family. The first is a remembered image of her family's car, with her father driving herself, her mother and brother recklessly toward their cabin, "plunging down over the elevator edges and scraping around the rockfaces," the children "getting sicker and sicker despite the Lifesavers their mother would hand out"(14). The second is a symbolic image of stuffed animals: "a father moose with a trench-coat and pipe in his mouth, and a little boy moose in short pants, a striped jersey and baseball cap, waving an American flag"; at some distance is the fourth family member, "a little girl moose in a frilly skirt and a pigtailed blonde wig, holding a red parasol in one hoof." Both images give us psychologically informative portraits of the protagonist's family – the first of an impatient father who values the efficiencies of speed, and a 'lifesaving' mother; the second a conventional North American family complete with sexual stereotypes and the eclipsing of girl by boy. The second is also, however, a lethally threatened family – as the real moose must have been before being killed, stuffed, and dressed in their bourgeois gear.

Like Marian MacAlpin, the narrator has, at most, superficial relationships with others. She says of Anna "she's my best friend, my best woman friend; I've known her two months." Of her lover Joe she says "I'm fond of him, I'd rather have him around than not; though it would be nice if he meant something more to me"(32). The source of these superficial relationships seems to lie partly in her vision of her childhood family – the girl moose separated from her 'happy' family. She remembers her mother mainly in terms of

Atwood's male image of the photographer, as an unemotional
woman who gathered "successive incarnations of me preserved and
flattened like flowers pressed in dictionaries"(69). She recalls her
botanist father as a rationalist who preferred animals to people –
"He didn't dislike people, he merely found them irrational; animals,
he said, were much more consistent, their behaviour at least was
predictable"(59). By implication, the father must have appeared to
prefer animals to his own daughter; certainly she is still seeking a
father when she becomes the lover of her art teacher, whose rationalism echoes that of the earlier man.

I worshipped him, non-child-bride, idolator, I kept the scraps of his
handwriting like saints' relics, he never wrote letters, all I had was the criticisms in red pencil he paperclipped to my drawings. Cs and Ds, he was an
idealist, he said he didn't want our relationship as he called it to influence his
aesthetic judgment. He didn't want our relationship to influence anything; it
was to be kept separate from life. (148-149)

When this relationship is ended by the rationalistic act of abortion
("he talked about it as though it was legal, simple, like getting a wart
removed") she is unable to speak of it to either parent, because of
their "innocence" – innocence, we guess, of the irrational, and of
their daughter.

   In *Lady Oracle,* the five-part structure of the novel, of which the
second focusses on Joan's childhood relationship with her mother
and father, effectively foregrounds the family as a source of Joan's
adult fantasies. A mother who is narcissistic and isolated makes it
difficult for the adult Joan ever to trust a woman-friend; a father who
is absent, shy, aloof, and who through military service and his work
as an anaesthetist has had power of life and death over others, leads
Joan into relationships with similarly aloof men to whom she metaphorically gives life-and-death power over herself. With both her
lover Paul and husband Arthur, she replicates her parents' drama of
unfulfilled self-absorbed and dependent woman married to an aloof
and undemonstrative man.

   It is by giving Rennie Wilford a single obsessively recurring childhood memory that Atwood emphasizes family relationships in
*Bodily Harm.* Three times Rennie's grandmother walks into her consciousness seeking "her hands." "I've left them somewhere and now
I can't find them," she says (57). Rennie's childhood response was
fear – "All I would think of at that time was how to get away from

Griswold.... I used to pray I wouldn't live long enough to get like my grandmother" (58). But she has. The grandmother has been her dominant parent.

One of the first things I can remember, says Rennie, is standing in my grandmother's bedroom. The light is coming in through the window, weak yellowish winter light, everything is very clean, and I'm cold. I know I've done something wrong, but I can't remember what. I'm crying. I'm holding my grandmother around both legs, but I didn't think of them as legs, I thought of her as one solid piece from the neck down to the bottom of her skirt. I feel as if I'm holding on to the edge of something, safety, if I let go I'll fall, I want forgiveness, but she's prying my hands away finger by finger. She's smiling; she was proud of the fact that she never lost her temper. (53)

This stern woman, who pries Rennie's "hands away finger by finger," has already lost symbolically the use of her own hands, lost compassion, long before she hallucinates their physical loss. She routinely shuts Rennie in the cellar as punishment, a cellar where "small things" move around, "small things that might get on you or run up your legs" (53). In consequence, Rennie herself grows up afraid to do wrong, afraid to be noticed, afraid to use her hands. "As a child I learned three things well, how to be quiet, what not to say, and how to look at things without touching them." Later as an adult she will look at the world without touching it, write in banal words that don't touch their subjects, enter 'love' relationships that barely touch the feelings of the lovers.

The emphasis which Atwood gives to passages in *Bodily Harm*, *Lady Oracle* and *Surfacing* which provide psychological sources for the adult behaviour of the protagonists suggests that to read the novels as structures of archetypal pattern rather than of human causation may be to misread them seriously. Archetypal patterns in these novels are circle games which trap characters into fruitlessly repetitive action, as Joan Foster is with her series of killer / healer men. These patterns enter the lives of the protagonists as acquired behaviours, learned from parents who have never dared to challenge the patterns inherited from their own parents. As Rennie Wilford says of the Victorian bric-a-brac handed down in her family, "It was understood that you could never sell these objects or give them away. The only way you could ever get rid of them was to will them to someone else and then die" (*BH* 54).

*

All the members of the family of *Surfacing*'s narrator are marked by the rationalist motif of collecting. The narrator's brother collects insects and small reptiles in jars; both children collect their drawings in scrapbooks which emulate the scrapbook in which their mother preserves their photographs. Later the narrator saves samples of her art teacher's handwriting, and her father collects Indian rock drawings. Like David with his movie camera, all are implicated in rationalism, in naming and arranging the nameless. Related to this motif is that of segmentation, categorization, dissection, and ultimately amputation. The narrator feels she has been "cut in two"(158). Her baby has been "sliced off from" her(48), has been taken out of her "with a fork like a pickle out of a pickle jar." She feels her "neck has closed over ... shutting me into my head." In the cabin of an abandoned workboat she has seen drawings of parts of her own body.

I was shocked, not by those parts of the body ... but that they should be cut off like that from the bodies that ought to have gone with them, as though they could detach themselves and crawl around on their own like snails.(119)

Segmentation is also a rationalist handling of reality to facilitate human control. It reduces a subject in size, allowing easier storage and manipulation – as in the botanical 'species' gathered by *Surfacing*'s drowned father. It divides a troublesome subject into portions which can be 'managed' outside the context of that subject – as the genitals above are separated from human individuality. The things 'segmented' in *Surfacing* are either those of nature – the heron, the landscape, the botanical specimens – or the narrator herself, who understandably in the climactic scenes of her breakdown identifies with the natural world. As in Atwood's poetry, ecology and feminist concern converge; woman's body becomes nature's body, fenced, confined to pattern, classified, 'amputated.'

In *Bodily Harm* amputation is a means of avoiding "massive involvement" – with cancer cells in the case of Rennie's illness, with human poverty and unhappiness in case of her 'lifestyle' articles. The surgical approach to life is portrayed here as neither a sufficient cure to illness nor a fulfilling way to human relationship. The full life involves "risk" – risk of cancer, risk of cockroaches, soiled clothes, limitation of 'options,' physical damage. "God forbid I should take a risk"(126) says Rennie in a rare moment of candid self-reproach.

The protagonist of *Surfacing*, reflecting on the amputation of repro-
duction from sexuality achieved by chemical birth control, remarks
bitterly "love without fear, sex without risk, that's what they wanted
to be true .... Love is taking precautions ..." (80).

*

Again Atwood has invoked a male versus female distinction. The
male approach to experience is legalistic (Peter the lawyer in *The
Edible Woman*), surgical (Daniel the cancer surgeon in *Bodily
Harm*), formulaic (Joan in *Lady Oracle*), superficial (David in *Surfacing*, Jake and Jocasta in *Bodily Harm*); the female is inclusive,
requires total 'involvement,' immersion, risk-taking, depth. The
male requires abrupt change, a severing of present from past, like
that attempted by Joan in her two escapes to Europe; the female, like
nature itself, requires evolution, transformation, the incorporation
of past into present.

... on the sodden trunks are colonies of plants, feeding on disintegration,
laurel, sundew the insect-eater, its toenail-sized leaves sticky with red hairs.
Out of the leaf nests the flowers rise, pure white, flesh of gnats and midges,
petals now, metamorphosis. (*S* 167)

This image of the sundew, seen by the protagonist of *Surfacing* just
before she begins her own descent to the protean depths of the lake,
personal history, and personal unconscious, is the basic image of all
four comic novels. Out of disorder grows new order, out of cancer
and suffering spiritual health, out of psychological collapse personal
wholeness. While the underlying structure of this process appears to
be that of comedy, Atwood's concern with metamorphosis alters the
comic pattern greatly. The individual is restored (with the exception
of Joan in *Lady Oracle*) not to order but to growth. The traditional
comic pattern is in a sense overturned; order becomes equated with
dehumanizing systematics, with ill-health, 'disorder'; traditional
disorder becomes organic process. The inherited pattern is seen, as it
were, through female eyes as something which merely confirms male
prejudices about stability and reason, and male fears about mutability and the irrational.

    The new pattern – for paradoxically the structural similarities
between the four novels imply both pattern and anti-pattern – is
closer to that of Freudian psychotherapy than to that of Jungian
archetype. Each character descends literally or symbolically into her

unconscious to locate previously repressed or 'amputated' materials which may allow the building of a new growth-oriented personality. In psychotherapy the subject descends to his unconscious to explore the fantasies, rationalizations, illusions, projections, and transferences which have distorted his vision of himself and his experiences – rationalizations similar to the fictions unconsciously manufactured by the narrator of *Surfacing* regarding her abortion.

... I couldn't accept it, that mutilation, ruin I'd made, I needed a different version, I'd pieced it together the best way I could, flattening it, scrapbook, collage, pasting over the wrong parts. A faked album, the memories fraudulent as passports. (143-144)

The psychoanalytic process is reductive, destructive. In *Surfacing* the overturning of the traditional comic pattern is echoed by the narrator's destruction of the false biography she has unconsciously created for herself; both are symbolized later in the narrator's ritual destruction of the dishes, books, and clothing in her parents' cabin. To her these things have become indelibly 'male' – paralytic, repressive, geometric, parts of the measured time of history. "Everything from history must be eliminated, the circles and the arrogant square pages," she tells us as she burns scrapbooks and photographs, slashes books, tents, blankets, and raincoats. Beyond these repressions, as in psychoanalysis, "everything is alien, everything is waiting to become alive"(159).

In *Lady Oracle* Joan Foster must similarly descend into the unconscious world of her transferences and projections, particularly her transference from her 'killer / healer' father to all the men of her life – Paul, the Royal Porcupine, the many-faced heroes of her Gothic romances, her turtle-necked husband Arthur.

Amazingly he began his transformations.... His face grew a white gauze mask, then a pair of mauve-tinted spectacles, then a red beard and mustache, which faded, giving place to burning eyes and icicle teeth. Then his cloak vanished and he stood looking at her sadly; he was wearing a turtle-neck sweater.

Her recognition is immediate and visibly 'reduces' the transference.

'No,' she said. 'I know who you are.'
The flesh fell away from his face, revealing the skull behind it; he stepped towards her, reaching for her throat. (343)

As in the Freudian theory of catharsis, when the neurosis is recognized, it should not only lose its power but also make way for long-stifled elements of the authentic self to grow. This pattern of increasingly conscious neurosis, reduction and simplification of the neurotic action, followed by tentative new growth is the true pattern of all these novels. Marian MacAlpin's unconscious fear of being devoured comes to the 'surface' of her consciousness as an increasing aversion to food and culminates in her realization that "what she really wanted ... had been reduced to simple safety." The realization takes place in a snowy ravine which her friend Duncan describes as "close to absolute zero," "as near as possible to nothing"(EW 263). When she returns to her apartment and decides to take her first positive action in several days – to bake a woman-shaped cake for Peter – it is with a marked sense of new personal beginning.

Her image was taking shape. Eggs. Flour. Lemons for the flavour. Sugar, icing-sugar, vanilla, salt, food-colouring. She wanted everything new, she didn't want to use anything that was already in the house. (267)

In Surfacing the protagonist experiences a similar 'surfacing' of unconscious elements – fear of people, books, enclosures, manufactured objects of all kinds – which reduces almost to zero not only her food but her access to warmth and shelter. From the beginning of this process, however, she experiences also the promise of "new meaning"(158), of death that springs "up from the earth, pure joy"(151). Her hallucinations bring her visions of her parents which seem to end her old dependencies on them.

Our father, our Mother, I pray, Reach down for me, but it won't work: they dwindle, grow, become what they were, human. Something I never gave them credit for; ...
I try to think for the first time what it was like to be them. (189-190)

When her hallucinations end, she feels free to "begin" life again, and to attempt a relationship with her previously undemonstrative lover Joe – "we can no longer live in peace by avoiding each other, the way it was before, we will have to begin"(192).

Rennie Wilford in Bodily Harm, despite the uncertainty which Atwood allows to surround her physical fate, clearly becomes new psychologically. Her haunting unconscious recollections of her senile grandmother's search for her 'hands,' her childhood memories of fearing to touch because of fearing to fail, culminate at the climax of the novel in her sudden acquiring of 'hands,' in her acquiring both the courage and the power to touch another. The girl who "could not bear to be touched" by the "groping" hands of her grandmother, who "puts her own hands away" and afterward dreams of herself handless, is enabled by her reclaiming of these lost memories not only to take the gravely injured Lora's hand in her own but to pull her back toward life.

She's holding Lora's left hand, between both of her own, perfectly still, nothing is moving, yet she knows she is pulling on the hand, as hard as she can, there's an invisible hole in the air, Lora is on the other side of it and she has to pull her through, she's gritting her teeth with the effort, she can hear herself, a moaning it must be her own voice, this is a gift, this is the hardest thing she's ever done.

She holds the hand, perfectly still, with all her strength. Surely, if she can only try hard enough, something will move and live again, something will get born. (299)

What will get born, what will "live again," may not be Lora but will be at least the essential 'touching' potential that is Rennie herself.

*

Only in *Lady Oracle* is the protagonist's renewal suspect. When Joan writes the final chapter of her Gothic novel "Stalked by Love," she undoubtedly recognizes the the unconscious patterns which have dominated her life. She has a particularly clear view of her pattern of passively waiting for the killer / healer to take her away, to "rescue" her, "a strong arm about her waist" (*LO* 343). Clear also to her is her tendency to flee from any crisis like a Gothic heroine, "climbing out a window, in my bibbed apron and bun, oblivious to the cries of the children and grandchildren behind me. I might as well face it, I thought, I was an artist, an escape artist" (335). She is indeed moved by her recognitions to new actions, not passively awaiting the next man to walk through her door but instead clubbing him with a Cinzano bottle. Unlike her old self, she also does not flee the consequences of this act.

I could have escaped; he wouldn't have been able to trace me. I'm surprised I didn't do that since I've always been terrified of being found out. But somehow I couldn't just run off and leave him in the hospital with no one to talk to; not after I'd almost killed him by mistake. (344)

But are these actions really new? Her attack with the Cinzano bottle is merely another instance of her fantasizing a man to be a Gothic villain; her decision to stay with and help her victim seems based not on a new sense of self but on the 'nurse' fantasy which patterned the novels of her first lover Paul: "he's a nice man; he doesn't have a very interesting nose, but I have to admit there is something about a man in a bandage ..."(345).

\*

Joan has also not freed herself of her breathless, anxious, and garrulous use of language. Wordiness is a characteristic of all four of Atwood's 'comic' protagonists – run-on sentences, imprecise diction, and in *The Edible Woman* and *Lady Oracle* giddy colloquialism. Their verbal wastefulness reverses the cryptic economy of Atwood's poetry, and in so doing provides an argument for that economy – that words belong to the surface world of manipulated and rationalized experience, that words conceal the 'underground' realities that are best communicated in code, in gestures rather than articulations of language. At the end of *Lady Oracle* Joan Foster is still relying on an unreliable medium; her anxiousness of speech, the wordiness of her explanations, comes from her intuitive sense that words will not serve her. She is drowning in language, wastes her energies against it in repetitive struggle.

As in the poetry, the elusive ideal in these novels is not only a female world prior to literary pattern but one prior to language itself. "Language," the narrator of *Surfacing* tells us, "divides us into fragments, I wanted to be whole"(146). Marian MacAlpin's retreat from a culture of segmented meat is in part a retreat from language – from "marriage manuals," "books on cameras," "law books," books "that told you how to work it" (150), from cookbooks with "diagrams of the planned cow," from meat "pre-packaged in cellophane, with name-labels and price-labels stuck on it." It is from language that divides and names. She begins to reject her job as "a manipulator of words" and to substitute prelinguistic symbols.

Marian looked at the clock. It was almost time for lunch. She drew a row of moons across her page: crescent moons, full moons, the crescent moon pointing the other way, then nothing: a black moon.... She got out of her chair ... she was tired, tired, tired of being a manipulator of words. (110)

Part of her attraction to Duncan lies in his suspicion of words ("Words ... are beginning to lose their meanings," he informs her) and in his preference for iconic messages, the pumpkin seed shells he leaves in the movie theatre "like some primitive signal, a heap of rocks or a sign made with sticks or notches cut in trees." When Marian bakes the woman-shaped cake at the novel's end she is using a similar signal, rejecting oral language in order to try to speak to Peter in the same medium in which she unconsciously receives messages from him – the medium of symbol, image, and iconic gesture.

All four protagonists have learned to dismiss what people say and to listen instead to the symbolism of their actions and possessions. Here is the woman of *Surfacing* 'listening' to her lover during their last lovemaking.

'I love you,' he says, into the side of my neck, catechism. Teeth grinding, he's holding back, he wants it to be like the city, baroque scrollwork, intricate as a computer.... (161)

Her rejection of language is the most emphatic in the novels. She begins to see without naming, her "eyes filtering the shapes, the names of things fading but their forms and uses remaining, the animals learned what to eat without nouns." The phenomenal world becomes semiotic, becomes "separate conversations"(150) new "languages."

The forest leaps upward, enormous, the way it was before they cut it, columns of sunlight frozen; the boulders float, melt, everything is made of water, even the rocks. In one of the languages there are no nouns, only verbs held for a long moment.
The animals have no need for speech, why talk when you are a word.

Significantly unnamed throughout the novel – in contrast to all the named and consequently less 'real' characters such as David, Anna, and Joe – the narrator herself now becomes a "word."

I lean against a tree, I am a tree leaning ... (181)

Later, when she imagines herself bearing a child with Joe, she says of the child she "will never teach it any words," and of Joe – who has throughout the book been taciturn, uncommunicative, "what will preserve him is the absence of words." Still later, realizing that as a human being she must inevitably use conventional speech, particularly in her relationship with Joe, it is the hopelessness of speech that she is most aware of.

> For us it's necessary, the intercession of words; and we will probably fail, sooner or later, more or less painfully. That's normal, it's the way it happens now and I don't know whether it's worth it.... (192)

*

> "You have the body of a goddess," the Polish Count used to say, in moments of contemplative passion. (Did he rehearse?)
> "Do I have the head of one too?" I replied archly.
> "Do not make such jokes," he said. "You must believe me. Why do you refuse to believe in your own beauty?"
> But which goddess did he mean? There was more than one, I knew. The one on the Venus pencil package, for instance, with no arms and all covered with cracks. Some goddesses didn't have bodies at all; there was one in the museum, three heads on top of a pillar, like a fire hydrant. Many were shaped like vases, many like stones. I found his compliment ambiguous. (LO 142)

As writers, both Joan Foster and Rennie Wilford are con-artists of language. Both, like Joan here, are acutely aware of its second order qualities, of its at best superficial correspondences with individual experience. Again and again in Atwood's novels second-order language empties a particular object, often a woman, of its specificity and makes it signify only a general idea.

> [The male sculptor] had one woman harnessed to a dogsled. It was called *Nationalism is Dangerous.* There was another one with a naked mannequin on her knees, chained to a toilet, with a Handy Andy between her teeth like a rose. It was called *Task Sharing,* said Frank.
> If a woman did that, said Rennie, they'd call it strident feminism. (BH 208)

But while Joan remains a victim of language, enslaved by its Gothic literary pattern of maiden on the run, Rennie's awareness of language's inadequacies and ambiguities increases: "*massive involvement,*" "*malignant,*" "*women like you*" (256) become messages of secret meaning. She slowly finds the authentic first-order meanings of the words shining through and destroying the second-order generalizations her culture has assigned to them. At the end of the novel the action of her hands becomes infinitely more powerful than spoken words, becomes, in fact, a means of returning the spoken word, the name, to authentic meaning.

> She holds the hand, perfectly still, with all her strength. Surely, if she can only try hard enough, something will move and live again, something will get born.
> "Lora," she says. The name descends and enters the body, there's something, a movement; isn't there? (299)

What is being born here, made to "live again," is not only Lora, not only Rennie's ability to 'touch'; it is language itself – it is naming. Rennie thus moves past the despair of the narrator of *Surfacing*; speech can be reconnected with the 'wordless' language of nature. Speech need not be the male Adamic naming of the pioneer or of Peter, David, the Count, or Jake. As in the crucial poem "Spelling" of *True Stories,* there can be a feminine naming, a feminine poetics, that speaks both in icons and in phonemes rooted in phenomena. "Lora," Rennie says.

A physical naming done by women: in *Bodily Harm* the hands of Rennie's mother touch those of her grandmother to ultimately become her own hands touching Lora and speaking her name. Authentic power and language pass in Atwood's fiction from woman to woman; in *Lady Oracle* what liberating knowledge Joan Foster possesses has come from her Aunt Lou; in *Surfacing* the crucial icons which free the narrator from the fake pattern of words she has invented about herself are preserved for her by her mother.

> My mother's gift was there for me, I could look.
> ... the gift was a loose page, the edge torn, the figures drawn in crayon. On the left was a woman with a round moon stomach; the baby was sitting up inside her gazing out. Opposite her was a man with horns on his head like cow horns and a barbed tail.
> The picture was mine, I had made it. The baby was myself before I was born, the man was God,....
> They were my guides, she had saved them for me, pictographs, I had to read their new meaning with the help of the power. (150)

Iconically, these pictures are outside of received pattern, "loose" from the book, "edges torn." They are not the denotative "symmetrically" drawn images of her other childhood drawings – "page after page of eggs and rabbits, grass and trees, normal and green, surrounding them, flowers blooming, sun in upper right hand corner of each picture, moon symmetrically in the left" – which echo society's 'happy family' view of marriage, sun loved by moon; these are primitive matriarchal images showing woman impregnated by Pan, by nature itself. When the narrator attempts, only a few pages later, to get pregnant by Joe, she is re-enacting these drawings, re-enacting her childhood image of her mother. Taking Joe to the tree-shrouded lakeshore, she has intercourse not with a specific man but with someone "thick, undefined, outline but no features, hair and beard a mane, moon behind him" – with one of the "nameless weeds" of nature.

CHAPTER FIVE

# Life Before Man

But she doesn't want to change position, she doesn't want to move. It might suggest to Nate the idea that he can move, that he is free to get up and walk out at any time. She knows – who better – that there is also that freedom, that exit. One way or another. Nate, on the contrary, has never discovered it. (*LBM* 261)

IN contrast to *The Edible Woman, Surfacing, Lady Oracle* and *Bodily Harm, Life Before Man* is relatively motionless in structure and action. The characters are unwilling to 'move,' like Elizabeth above, unaware of the possibility of movement, like her husband Nate, or fearful of moving like Nate's new companion Lesje. While the characters manage to alter their living arrangements during the novel, they do not gain any liberating insight into their own lives, nor greatly change how they feel about their lives. One of our last images of Nate, whom we were told in the second chapter "wants to do something, perform something"(17), reveals him trying to jog around Toronto's Queen's Park Circle. There is a double irony here, for not only does the circle suggest, as in *The Circle Game,* a structure closed to change, but Nate fails even to complete it. He walks north to meet Lesje at the Royal Ontario Museum, where both she and his estranged wife Elizabeth work. There, another circle is completed as Nate waits for Lesje "in the same spot he used to wait for Elizabeth, one shoulder against the stone"(314). Two signs on the museum, which is being renovated, compete for his attention: "THE PLANETARIUM IS STILL OPEN" says one, suggesting the open 'exit' Nate has still not recognized. "ROM Wasn't Built in a Day" says the other, expressing the pessimism that has coloured all of Nate's life. Needless to say, Nate, for whom the introspective Lesje is merely another unpredictable and potentially demanding woman like the angry Elizabeth before her, attends only to the second sign. "Another worthy cause," he thinks. "They'll suck him dry despite his sawdust heart"(314).

81

*

The narrative structure of *Life Before Man* echoes the stillness of the characters' lives. In contrast to the unified narrative points of view and the large sections of continuous narrative of the other four novels, *Life Before Man* is related from three perspectives in small chapters of narrative that detail the events of only thirty-four days of a three-year period. Many of the days are presented in three successive chapters, from each of Nate's, Elizabeth's, and Lesje's perspectives; here time virtually ceases. The organizing principle of the novel is not continuous narrative but the chapter module. The emphasis is on the quality of individual days, and on the similarities between their events, rather than on evolving situations. Much like the discontinuous stanzas of Atwood's poetry, the chapters appear as independent, discrete units which juxtapose in a nearly static structure rather than merge into a developing shape. When on the final page Elizabeth finds herself overcome by a display of idealized paintings of life in contemporary China, with "turnips in the innocent rows, ordinary, lit from within, the praise lavished on mere tomatoes, the bunches of grapes, painted in all their translucent hues," and resignedly leaves to view grapes in a supermarket (while Atwood observes "China does not exist. Nevertheless she longs to be there"), we feel the novel could easily continue to present similar scenes of longing and resignation for another hundred pages. The characters' lives have reached not even partial resolution, and seem unlikely to do so. For all three characters, the novel has barely moved past its opening lines, in which Elizabeth declared,

I don't know how I should live. I don't know how. I don't know how anyone should live. All I know is how I do live. (11)

*

Paradoxically, the subconscious "green world" of Atwood's other novels is very much present in *Life Before Man*. All three major characters are presented in considerable psychological depth; all three re-evaluate the shaping events of their childhood and consider the extent to which they have allowed these events to have deterministic control over their present lives.

Lesje feels haunted by her contradictory Jewish and Ukrainian families, by a Jewish aunt who was murdered by Nazis and a Ukrainian grandfather who welcomed Hitler, a Ukrainian grandmother who once gave her "one of the untouchable decorated eggs" and a Jewish grandmother who "had smashed the egg with her tiny boots"(66), by a Jewish father who changed his family name from Etlin to Green, and a Ukrainian mother who named her "Lesje" after "a famous Ukrainian poet whose poems Lesje would never be able to read." Feeling alien to both heritages, Lesje had by grade five claimed geology and its conflict-free "language" as "something personal from her own life."

The names [of rocks] were a language; not many people might know it, but if you found one who did, you would be able to talk together.... 'Schist,' she would say, 'magma, igneous, malachite, pyrite, lignite.' The names of the dinosaurs, when she found out about them, were even more satisfactory.

Ultimately, she constructs an elaborate fantasy life about being the only human in "Jurassic swamps," and invests it with nearly all of her emotions. Here she is safe – "so totally alien" to the dinosaurs that they are not "able to focus on her"(18) – and free of the petty sectarian world of "other human beings"(18). She sees herself in the recurrent Atwood image of "tourist or refugee"(19), and becomes indifferent about her own species.

Does she care whether the human race survives or not. She doesn't know. The dinosaurs didn't survive and it wasn't the end of the world.

Lesje's dinosaurs serve two metaphoric functions. Primarily they stand for the warring sides of her family, 'dinosaurs' from a European past irrelevant to her Canadian present. Preoccupied by the past, the family members are, like the dinosaurs, unable "to focus" on Lesje, and make her feel "totally alien." Yet clearly the dinosaurs also stand as relief from family, as somehow more humane companions who will consistently allow Lesje an undisturbed existence. They provide her with a fantasy 'life before man' which delivers her from a human race she has experienced, through her family, only in terms of cruelty and interference.

Nate feels similarly controlled by his childhood experiences. His soldier father had died in England during the Second World War, making him feel "overshadowed." "It's hard to compete with any dead man ... much less a hero"(33). His mother had worked for idealistic causes – "the Korean poets, the crippled vets"(285) – for as long as Nate could remember, and had taken him to the Unitarian church with its "idealistic hymns about the brotherhood of man." He had felt smothered all his life by what he saw as his mother's idealism,

The weight of her ideal son presses on his chest, a plaster mannequin
threatening to enter and choke him. (285)

He transfers this feeling to all the women in his life,

Years of her moral smugness, burying him like snow, like layers of wool.
Intolerable smugness of all of them, Elizabeth, his mother, even Lesje.... He
knows that silent equation, he's been well-schooled: *I suffer, therefore I am
right.*

Driven more by a compulsion to measure up to women's expectations than by his own desires, Nate has continually felt judged by
women. "You've always been afraid of being a horse's ass," his
mother tells him. "Even as a child" (286).

   In Elizabeth, Atwood presents yet a third character whose life is
dominated by dramas from her family past. Like Lesje, she feels herself to be a "refugee" (150) – from both her parents' drunken and
careless poverty and her Aunt Muriel's strict gentility. Her father,
perpetually out of work and with overt sexual feelings toward her,
moves the family each time the rent is due and finally deserts altogether. Her mother, characterized by "helplessness" (131) during
and after the marriage, becomes a skid-road derelict and dies from
burns suffered as a result of her own careless smoking and drinking.
Elizabeth's wealthy aunt Muriel takes her and her sister from the
mother's apartment during one of the mother's many absences following the father's desertion. In Aunt Muriel's Rosedale mansion,
Elizabeth finds another weak man, Uncle Teddy, who like her father
makes mild paedophiliac advances to her. More importantly, she
absorbs Aunt Muriel's hostility to men and to weakness, together
with her sternly defensive posture to the world.

Auntie Muriel worked at developing those parts of Elizabeth that most
resembled Auntie Muriel and suppressing or punishing the other parts. Auntie Muriel admired backbone, and Elizabeth feels that, underneath everything, she now has the backbone of a rhinoceros. (137)

The consequences of this background for Elizabeth are numerous
and varied. For one thing, she is attracted only to men – her
highschool pickups, her husband Nate, her lover Chris – whom she
can dominate and discard, much the way Aunt Muriel dominated
and psychologically discarded Uncle Teddy. For another, she feels

perpetually homeless, and has dreams of her two daughters being kidnapped much the way she and her sister were taken by Aunt Muriel. Certainly she feels she has Aunt Muriel's "backbone of a rhinoceros," but she also despises Aunt Muriel – tries actively from her early teens to repudiate her sexual prohibitions. Further, this "backbone" does not prevent her from experiencing profound guilt for having denied her mother, or feelings of "worthlessness" for having descended from a woman who spent any money she ever had on liquor. She has wishful fantasies of her mother as a rescuing 'Glinda the Good' from L. Frank Baum's *The Wizard of Oz*(139), or as "a saint under the street lights"(281).

*

... Elizabeth cannot forgive. She cannot forgive her own treachery. (289)

Despite the fact that all three characters know the critical events in their pasts, despite their spending many chapters mulling these events over, and despite their understanding – particularly in the cases of Nate and Elizabeth – the actual mechanisms by which they unfairly transfer feelings from parent to lover, or by which they actively seek mates who resemble Nate's mother and Elizabeth's father respectively, only Lesje achieves a somewhat changed attitude to life. While the other four novels used psychological understanding for a cathartic breakthrough to new hope, this novel uses it largely to confirm the continuing power of the past. The characters here take few risks, refuse the deconstructive cathartic act – refuse to smash objects or relationships, or to descend into madness or exile. Their insights into themselves are thus restricted to conventional language, to the rational, and are never transmitted to their irrational selves, to the pre-linguistic underground of their biological energies.

Consequently *Life Before Man,* unlike *The Edible Woman, Surfacing, Lady Oracle,* and *Bodily Harm,* has no climactic moment. Marian MacAlpin sees the new snow of the Rosedale Valley and resolves to bake her cake; *Surfacing*'s narrator meets the corpse of her father face to face under the water and begins to learn at last her place in nature; Joan Foster penetrates the heart of the Gothic maze and learns at least the secret transferences which have determined the course of her life so far; Rennie Wilford watches Lora beaten almost to death by prison guards and finds her own hands restored to use. These climaxes give each character a sense of deep change, and conviction that something new awaits them. In *Life Before Man* such insight neither comes via traumatic event nor carries with it any promise of redemption. Even Lesje's fantasy life – which resembles Marian's fantasies about food, the *Surfacing* narrator's fantasy about 'voice' in nature, and Joan's fantasies about Gothic adventure – is mostly barren of instruction.

\*

I had to do something to keep myself alive. (286)

Thus says Nate's mother when, still half-believing in her idealistic devotion to various social causes, he asks her to explain why she has actively supported them. Doing "something to keep ... alive" – minimal survival – is the main achievement of the characters in *Life Before Man*. In this particular scene Nate's discovery that his mother worked for such things as the war veterans and the Unitarian church merely to avoid despair and "potential suicide"(287) relieves him of the burden of being an "ideal son" and allows him to continue running, if only around Queen's Park Circle. Minimal survival – carrying on even when one's course is not clear – is also Lesje's accomplishment after having deliberately risked becoming pregnant.

... pushing in whether she wants it to or not, is what Marianne would call her life. It's possible she's blown it. This is what they mean when they say *maturity* – you get to the point where you think you've blown your life ... but she isn't sorry.

True, there's a chance she's done a stupid thing. Several, many. Or she may have done a wise thing for a stupid reason. (311)

At the heart of this accomplishment is the fact she has "done" at least a "thing," no matter whether "stupid" or "wise." Such survival is even accomplished by Elizabeth:

At home they'll change their clothes and she'll make them something. Peanut butter sandwiches.

It suddenly amazes her that she is able to do this, something this simple. (301)

What *Life Before Man* leaves its characters with is respect for their own small successes. Considering the various traumas of Elizabeth's family background, even having two children, having made a home for two children, having sandwiches for these children, are minor triumphs.

But she's alive, she walks around, she holds down a job even. She has two children. (301)

*

On the spur of the moment she decided to kill herself. (292)

In *Life Before Man* there is no redemption of the past for its characters; there is only the option of taking responsibility for their own struggles, of seeing themselves as potential causes of relatively small events – perhaps only of a peanut butter sandwich. The alternative throughout the novel is suicide. The example of the self-destruction of Elizabeth's lover Chris hangs over the book, tempting Nate on at least two occasions, tempting Elizabeth during her aunt's funeral, and tempting Lesje above. But it hangs over the book not just as a resolution to despair; it also hangs over it as a challenge – a challenge to affirm life with recklessness, extravagance. Chris is the character in *Life Before Man* with the greatest number of the disorderly "underground" qualities one expects in Atwood's writing. Dramatically, his life opposes the cautious, pragmatic and essentially closed lives led by the other characters. He drives an old convertible that lacks a muffler. He parks "illegally" on almost every occasion – to the puzzlement of part-time lawyer Nate. He plays chess "like a Cossack" in contrast to Nate's "grouping his men in tight clumps, taking no chances" (173). He rebels against the genteel rules for extramarital sex laid down by Elizabeth – the schedule of Saturday nights for Nate and Thursday for herself, her insistence that the routines of the household be never disturbed by impromptu phone calls or visits. He yearns to sabotage the polite and genteel, pretending to be of Indian or Metis blood, taunting Nate with evidence of Elizabeth's infidelity, pressing Elizabeth to break up her bourgeois household to live with him. Ultimately he commits the greatest impropriety of all – shooting his head off with a shotgun. Even this act is designed by him to be angry, deconstructive. He dresses himself in white shirt, tie, a suit, polished shoes in a parody of the gentleman Elizabeth wished him to be. Nate, who has consistently misread Chris as a potential murderer (Nate tends to see any passion as dangerous), misreads his death too as an act of despair at his inability to reason.

The head had always been a troublemaker, which was probably why Chris had chosen to shoot at it instead of at some other part of himself. He wouldn't have wanted to mutilate his body. (16)

In fact Chris seems to have directed this shot against the 'gentleman,' against the head as symbol for the rationalism and passionless systematizing which Elizabeth prized. He has left his body not in vanity but in irony – to Elizabeth who had used but never acknowledged it, who had kept it as separate from her everyday life as it is now separate from his head.

\*

There's a toy he [Nate] once made, a favourite several years back, lathe work, a wooden man built of rings which slipped over a central post. The head screwed on, holding the man together. A clown's smile he used. This is his body, stiff fragments held together by his spine and his screwtop head. Segmented man. (244)

The central paradox of *Life Before Man* is that Chris's suicide is both the most life-affirming act of the book and its most life-denying. It effectively ends Chris's possibilities for a richer life while causing small changes within the lives of customarily passive Elizabeth, Nate, and Lesje. As a bitter parody of Elizabeth's penchant for 'amputating' sex from the rest of life, it repeats the head-body imagery of the other novels and argues again that the full life is the integrated life in which the 'underground' body has been allowed to 'surface' into the consciousness of head. Chris's work as a taxidermist, restoring the appearance of life to dead bodies, is metaphorically the task he tried to carry out with Elizabeth. In death he becomes a sacrificial hero, a 'hanged man,' whose dying opens the way for the small changes the remaining characters achieve.

\*

Chris says nothing. He's leaning in the doorway, smiling: a rat smile, lip lifted back over yellowed teeth. Nate doesn't feel like turning his back on him to go to the kitchen for glasses, but he can hardly walk backwards. Late-movie scenarios unreel: himself conked with a brass candle-stick or one of Elizabeth's heavy bowls, left unconscious in the hallway; the children kidnapped, held hostage, barricaded and terrified in Chris's two-roomed hideaway while Chris hunches over his chessboard like the Phantom of the Opera and the police megaphone from doorways; Elizabeth dumped bruised and naked in a culvert, bedsheet knotted round her neck. (235)

On most occasions when Chris appears in the novel the version we are given of him is Nate's version, a fantasy character into whom

Nate projects all the violence he has repressed in himself. He makes Chris into his black twin, animalistic where Nate is civilized, violent where he is pacifistic, decisive where he is hesitant, possessive toward Elizabeth where he is acquiescent.

... she'll disappear down the front walk, ass first, slung over Chris's shoulder, pencils and keys tumbling from her purse. Maybe she would like that, Nate thinks. (236)

We cannot trust this version any more than we can trust Elizabeth's reading of Chris when they first make love in his workroom, "his cold zipper ... pressed into the flesh of her inner thigh, the teeth rasping," as someone totally primitive, "liquid and rich"(74). For Elizabeth he is merely another incarnation of the 'dangerous' man who can give her violent sex – "like a car crash ... violence, metal on metal" (179) – who has the "latent power" "she knows she can control."(178)

The only reliable pieces of information we are given about Chris are the things he is associated with. As in Atwood's poetry, icons and symbols speak to us where discursive language fails. The symbols are not only those of openness and defiance of regulation – his convertible car, its missing muffler, his illegal parking, but of decay – "a smell like ... the inside of old cupboards, mousy, secretive, like musk, dusky and rich"(25) and of disorder – "the scraps of fur, shavings of wood"(74) of his Royal Ontario Museum workroom, the impression of "nothing ... in the right place" of his apartment (174). When he comes to ask Nate to help him persuade Elizabeth to marry him, "his hands dangle heavily from the sleeves of his crumpled corduroy jacket"(234). Unlike Elizabeth or Nate, he cannot bother to observe forms, keep up appearances, pretend confidence when his body wishes to go "slinking across the street like a straggler from a defeated army"(236). These images connect with other positive images in Atwood's fiction – the swamp images of Surfacing, Duncan's unkempt appearance in The Edible Woman, Lora's earthy practicality in Bodily Harm.

Chris's difficulty is that he is an integrated person in a society of segmented heads and bodies. His feelings express themselves in his posture and walk. His error with Elizabeth is not to be overly possessive of her but to misread her sexual response to him as a personal response, to misread someone who has segmented the various parts of her life, who considers him "only a vacation"(161), for someone as whole as himself.

*

It's the rule that when Elizabeth cooks, Nate does the dishes. One of the
many rules, subrules, codicils, addenda, errata. Living with Elizabeth
involves a maze of such legalities, no easier to understand because some of
them are unspoken. (163)

*Life Before Man* thus makes exceedingly clear the fact that Atwood's
male versus female dichotomy of order versus disorder, solid versus
liquid, stasis versus process, segmentation versus wholeness, is a
metaphor, rather than a literal distinction between men and women.
It is a feminist vision of nature rather than of politics. The most
vigorous manifestation of female force in *Life Before Man* is Chris,
who acts as if his fellow men and women had not split the world into
the legal and illegal, the polite and impolite, the job and the "vacation." The most 'male' of *Life Before Man* is Elizabeth, whose chief
delight is 'control,' whose job is the arranging of museum displays,
who maintains her body like "servicing a car, keeping it well cleaned,
its moving parts in trim, ready for the time when she might be able to
use it ..." (85). When she says her final angry words to Chris, they
strike him like a solid meeting a liquid, like a gunshot meeting flesh.

'Get out' is all she says.... Chris has turned, his face folding, pleating itself
like water hit by a rock.

As he leaves, the images Atwood gives Elizabeth are closed — "her
mouth set" and her gestures systematic:

... he's gone. There is only Elizabeth, her mouth set in that tight line of
displeasure, pulling her leather gloves off finger by finger. (236)

Nate, whose quitting work as a lawyer to build hand-made wooden
toys in his basement would seem to qualify him as a participant in
female energy, is portrayed by Atwood as self-deceived. He may have
rejected law because it uses "a language deliberately dried so that it
was empty of any sensuous values" but has chosen to build toys only
because society currently believes "physical objects ... to have a
magic, a mysterious aura ... superior to politics or law." He seeks
approval from all around him, and visualizes women, even the
socially maladroit Lesje, as sources of order and competence for his
unconfident self. His inability to control his life does not result from
a committment to 'underground' force; it results from his passivity,
indecisiveness, and incompetence. His fantasy vision of Chris

betrays a repressed self as violent and brutal as that assigned to any man in Atwood's writing. His fear that Chris may strangle Elizabeth is an open announcement of what he would like to do to her himself.

\*

Pervading *Life Before Man* is the symbol of the Royal Ontario Museum where Chris, Lesje, and Elizabeth all work to restore the semblance of life to the bodies of the dead. The museum is the ultimate rationalizer of natural force, cataloguing and categorizing the wonders of the past, and demystifying the present.

Elizabeth, shivering, stares up at the sky, which isn't really a sky but a complicated machine with tiny lights projected by slides and push-buttons. People do not become stars of any kind when they die. Comets do not really cause plagues. Really there is nobody in the sky. Really there is no round sphere of darkness, no black sun, no frozen silver man. (78)

The repetitive tasks of organization – the cataloguing of "giant tortoises from the Lower Cretaceous," of hundreds of "fish earbones from the Miocene"(182), that Lesje finds so meaningless, echo the systematization that characterizes Elizabeth's personal life and even Nate's ideal of doing "one thing well" – which he quickly defines as having "a monthly balance sheet"(43). Lesje's dissatisfaction with her work and her frequent escape into her Jurassic fantasies mark her like Chris with 'underground' or 'female' allegiances. The dry bones of the museum are not enough for her.

*Live again!* she'd wanted to cry, like some Old Testament prophet, like God, throwing up her arms, willing thunderbolts; and the strange flesh would grow again, cover the bones, the badlands would moisten and flower. (80-81)

Her way of achieving this metamorphosis (an image which also connects with the protean swampland of *Surfacing*), in a society committed to reason, politeness, and ceremony, is to revivify the Jurassic in her mind, where she can defy the reasonable – "she mixes eras, adds colours, why not a metallic blue Stegosaurus with red and yellow dots instead of the dull grey and brown postulated by the experts."

Outside of her fantasies Lesje also breaks the rules. She lacks social polish and talent for small talk, she spills her drinks at parties, makes conversational blunders, is as inept at creating the 'correct' surfaces of clothing, furniture and behaviour as Elizabeth is adept. Through these signals Atwood tells us she is the most redeemable character of the novel, and foreshadows her ultimate rule-breaking of discarding her birth control pills in order to claim her future. Unlike Chris, she finds a way beyond suicide to reject good taste, to reject rationalism, and assert her protean reality. She finds herself taking action in her life almost despite herself, impulsively flushing the pills down the toilet and at last moving toward bearing the child she has so long wanted. She finds the feeling of having acted surprising – "She's not used to being a cause, of anything at all" (310). She finds she has lost the ability to conjure up her dinosaur fantasies, and alone among all the characters finds herself seeing "new images," Staring at the Royal Ontario Museum's dinosaur fossils and hoping to reawaken her Jurassic daydreams, she discovers

... she can't do it. Either she's lost faith or she's too tired; at any rate she can no longer concentrate. The fragments of new images intrude. She looks down at the pebbles, the bark chips, the dusty cycad trees on the other side of the ledge, a thousand miles away.

The birth control pills – the "green plastic dial-a-pill dispenser" repeat the "green plastic packages, moon-shaped" of similar pills in *Surfacing*; Lesje's seeking pregnancy without Nate's knowledge reiterates the choice of the narrator of *Surfacing* to enter the future through independently-sought childbearing, to re-invent herself through giving birth to a child. Both birth images connect with Rennie's hope to cause Lora to "get born" again in *Bodily Harm*. As in the earlier novels, a woman's independent committment to new life creates a symbolic break with the past; here it ends Lesje's museum-dependent fantasies – and leads to "new" images, a chance to "begin" (311). Despite the slow, almost static pace of *Life Before Man*, its hidden narrative pattern is apparently still the earlier one of metamorphosis – but now itself metamorphosed into a new, nearly minimal, form.

CHAPTER SIX

# An Atwood Vocabulary
Technological Skin, Mirrors, The Gothic, Refugees and Tourists,
Underground Mazes, Metamorphosis, Signposts / Totems

---

## Technological Skin
... raw wires dangled like loose nerves from most of the sockets. (*EW* 57)

In Atwood's writing images from technology are invariably associated with the time-fixing attempt to suppress or replace nature. In *The Edible Woman* Peter is associated not only with the camera, but with guns, hunting magazines, "a doctor's examination table"(149), and with an automobile which he uses as a weapon to chase and capture Marian.

He glanced quickly over at me, his eyes narrowed as though he was taking aim. Then he gritted his teeth together and stepped murderously on the accelerator. (81)

Peter is also associated, however, with attempts to replace nature – as, for example, in Atwood's description of the modernistic apartment building still under construction, in which he lives. The building is portrayed as a ghoulish technological mimicking of a living organism, complete with nerves, sockets, skin, and shell.

Inside, the shiny surfaces – tiled floors, painted walls, mirrors, light-fixtures – which would later give the building its expensive gloss, its beetle-hard internal shell, had not yet begun to secrete themselves. The rough grey underskin of subflooring and plastered wall-surfaces was still showing, and raw wires dangled like loose nerves.... (57)

In *Surfacing* the fake art of David's film "Random Samples" is linked both to the motorized movie-camera and to the city with its "bus stations" and "acid taste of copper wiring" and its inhabitants who are "evolving ... halfway to machine"(183-184). In *Life Before Man* the simplistic technological view of the world is dramatized in William, an ecologist, in his optimistic view that "every catastrophe is merely a problem looking for a brilliant solution" (28). William is attracted to Lesje because she can "use technical language in front of his

93

friends. It gives him a hard-on when she says Pleistocene"(29). Here technology triggers what was once a purely biological response.

In Atwood's poetry such images tend to be less developed. The manipulative lover in "A Meal" is said to speak with a "metallic clink," to have a mind that smells "of insecticide"(CG 33-34). One of the few poems dominated by technological imagery is "Three Desk Objects," where a lamp, a typewriter, and a clock are shown to have taken on the biological qualities of Peter's apartment building.

... my electric typewriter
with your cord and hungry plug
drinking a sinister transfusion
from the other side of the wall

Like Marian MacAlpin, the speaker finds this apparent invasion of biology by technology a frighteningly Gothic event.

I am afraid to touch you
I think you will cry out in pain

I think you will be warm, like skin.
(PU 44)

## Mirrors

If ... the viewer is given a mirror that reflects not him but someone else, and told at the same time that the reflection he sees is himself, he will get a very distorted idea of what he really is like. (Su 16)

The mirror in Atwood's writing is deceptive, or as the poem "Tricks with Mirrors" tells us, "crafty." It invariably invokes the Narcissus legend ; it is a false pond, something to be treated as water rather than glass, to be plunged through into otherness rather than allowed to shine back the self. If believed to be glass, it reflects at worst a false, often reversed image, and further distorts a character's already weak sense of identity as in The Edible Woman where it contributes to Marian's sense that her body is being enveloped in 'technological skin.'

Finally Ainsley took a lipstick-brush and painted the mouth with several coats of glossy finish. 'There,' she said, holding a handmirror so that Marian could see herself....

Marian stared into the egyptian-lidded and outlined and thickly-fringed eyes of a person she had never seen before. She was afraid even to blink, for fear that this applied face would crack and flake with the strain. (EW 222)

At best, the 'glass' mirror's accurate reflecting of the character places him in a closed universe, bounded by the two unchanging versions of himself. Usually it is Atwood's male characters who have this Narcissus relationship to the mirror, and the women characters who have their identity confused by it.

In *The Edible Woman* the mirror is presented as part of Peter's world of gun, car, and camera, as one of the instruments by which Marian may be coerced into his world. The newly installed mirrors of the apartment building make "the lobby seem larger, much longer than it really was"(225). The mirrors beside the Park Plaza hotel elevators seek to persuade Marian that she can be one more matching accessory to Peter's "functional" body.

> While we waited for the elevator I watched our double image in the floor-to-ceiling mirror by the elevator doors. Peter was wearing one of his more subdued costumes, a brownish-green summer suit whose cut emphasised the functional sparseness of his body. All his accessories matched.
>     'I wonder if Len's up there yet,' I said to him, keeping an eye on myself and talking to him in the mirror. I was thinking I was just about the right height for him. (65)

While the options these mirrors offer are closed, restricting ones, the closure can only be achieved by Marian's accepting what she sees in the mirror. In the case of the man in "The Circle Game," the reflected image seems to be accurate, and the closure already achieved. The man's challenge is not to avoid acknowledging a false image, but to live in the ongoing moment with the woman rather than in a static, reflexive relationship with the mirror.

> You look past me ...
> watching
> your own reflection somewhere
> behind my head,
> over my shoulder (CG 37)

We are told that while the man does not wish to be merely his "exact reflection" in a mirror, he "yet will not walk from the glass, be separate." Like the man in *Power Politics* narcissistically in love more with his heroic or romantic images of himself than with the narrator, this man seems usually more fascinated by his own game-playing expertise than by the woman whom he claims to want.

Atwood's most detailed portrait of the narcissistic lover occurs in "Tricks with Mirrors," in which a woman observes herself becoming only a mirror to her lover. For the narcissist "Mirrors / are the perfect lover," reflecting back the "closed and perfect self" he believes himself to be. "Fall into me," the narrator tells him,

it will be your own
mouth you hit, firm and glassy

your own eyes you find you
are up against        closed        closed. (*YAH* 24)

The woman in such a relationship, having become the mirror, is of course painfully constricted and reduced. She lives in a "frame" with "limits / and reflections of its own." "A nail in the back" of the frame along with other nails suggests a crucifixion-like martyrdom.

pay attention to the nail
marks in the wood

they are important too. (*YAH* 25)

To "preserve" his image within her she must give up all expression of personal feeling.

Consider what restraint it

takes: breath withheld, no anger
or joy disturbing the surface
of the ice. (*YAH* 26)

The female portrait here is of a woman who is unexplainably dependent on the man, who can live only for him and who must reflect back to him only what he wishes to see. Nowhere is there evidence of why she might wish the relationship to continue. Toward the end of the poem she suggests that her experience is more that of being "trapped behind a door" than that of being mirror, that she needs him "to say the releasing word." Both the door image and the mirror image, of course, depict a woman who is mysteriously dependent on the man. As in "The Circle Game," the man has no positive qualities which would explain the woman's attraction to him, or malevolent ones which would explain his power over her. Why should she have to wait for him "to say the releasing word"? In "Tricks with

Mirrors," however, the woman seems eventually to notice the possibility of her own freedom.

Perhaps I am not a mirror.
Perhaps I am a pool.

The pool would be 'female,' natural and changeable, unlike the helpless 'male' glass of the mirror. It would open into the underground, into the otherness of both her own identity and unexpected event.

To dissolve glass mirror into liquid pool, or at least to deny the mirror its control of one's self, is a major struggle for the women protagonists of both *Surfacing* and *Lady Oracle*. The narrator of *Surfacing*, like the narrator of "Tricks with Mirrors," sees the mirror as a potential trap, as a source of both "distortion" and limited "vision."

I must stop being in the mirror. I look for the last time at my distorted glass face: eyes light blue in dark red skin, hair standing tangled out from my head, reflection intruding between my eyes and vision. Not to see myself but see. I reverse the mirror toward the wall, it no longer traps me, Anna's soul closed in the gold compact.... (175)

Again the mirror offers a "closed" temporally limited version of the self reminiscent of the sculptural "world of glass, / hard marble, carven word" of *Double Persephone*. The person who defines herself by her image in the mirror enters into a timeless "compact"; having defined herself by her past, she will find the mirror continually reflecting that definition back upon her. The narrator denies Narcissus's wish, "to see myself," preferring to see beyond the mirror into the evolving present.

The narrator's way to see 'beyond' is to turn from mirror to lake, to plunge into the lake to a new vision of the natural world, of her parents, and of her own life. The mirror here stands not only for individual narcissism but for cultural narcissism – for the cultural propensity to look at nature and see only human need, to look at a tree and see lumber, at a fish and see food, at a blue heron and see sport. Only by plunging through the humanistic mirror can one perceive the otherness of nature, its indifference to human purpose, the separateness of its will.

Atwood makes the need to see beyond or behind the mirror, to treat the mirror as 'pool,' even clearer in *Lady Oracle*. All her life Joan Foster has been plagued by the images reflected back to her both by real mirrors and by the metaphorical mirrors of billboards, movies, and magazine advertising. As an overweight child in a ballet costume, she is confronted in the mirror by both her bloated shape and the disfiguring lines of her own tears.

My made-up face had run, there were black streaks down my cheeks like sooty tears and my purple mouth was smudged and swollen. (49-50)

As a slim adult, Joan receives the same message.

When I looked in the mirror, I didn't see what Arthur saw. The outline of my former body still surrounded me ... like the image of Dumbo the Flying Elephant.... (214)

Joan finds the images she sees reflected in the popular media equally persuasive; as she says, "I'd always found other people's versions of reality very influential"(160). When she sees the movie *The Red Shoes*, for example, she identifies totally with the characterization of the ballerina.

I adored her: not only did she have red hair and an entrancing pair of red satin slippers to match, but she also had beautiful costumes, and she suffered more than anyone. I munched faster and faster as she became more entangled in her dilemma – I wanted those things too, I wanted to dance and be married to a handsome orchestra conductor, both at once.... (82)

One of Joan's major tasks in this book is to look past the various mirror images that confront her, to separate herself from the reflected image. She does this by literally going "into the mirror" while experimenting with automatic writing. These experiences in which she sat with a candle before a triple mirror gave her "the sense of going along a narrow passage that led downward"(221). What we see here is the journey past narcissism and the derivative image into the subconscious self. The journey is similar to the plunge the narrator of *Surfacing* takes into both the lake and into her unconscious; the destination is elsewhere called by Atwood "under the surface," as in "This is a Photograph of Me," or "underground."

## The Gothic
Once behind the mirror, or behind the photograph, or under the surface of picturesque nature, we may see unsettling and unwanted things. The descending corridor leads Joan Foster to darkness and suffocation, the Ontario bush teaches Susanna Moodie to

... take care
to look behind, within
where the skeleton face beneath

the face puts on its feather mask, the arm
within the arm lifts up the spear: (*JSM* 37)

Such subterranean threats and horrors belong to the literary Gothic, most familiar to the twentieth-century in films such as *The Exorcist*, *Jaws*, *Poltergeist*, or *Rosemary's Baby*, a genre in which a threat comes variously from primitive, underground, underwater, or subconscious sources. The Gothic in literature dates from the romantic medievalism of the late eighteenth century and refers specifically to the novels of mystery, intrigue, and supernatural horror, usually set in medieval crypts and dungeons, to which this medievalism gave birth. Characterizations in these novels, usually much weaker than the elaborate settings of trap doors, subterranean passages, ghosts, and animated suits of armour, depend on simplistic oppositions between good and evil. The oppositions often – as in the case of the monster of Mary Shelley's novel *Frankenstein* – occur within the same figure. Atwood's interest in the Gothic novel dominated her graduate studies at Harvard, and has since been openly expressed in poems like "Speeches for Dr. Frankenstein," in her essay on H. Rider Haggard "Superwoman Drawn and Quartered: The Early Forms of *She*,"[1] and in interviews such as one with J.R. Struthers in which she labels *Lady Oracle* an "anti-Gothic" based partly on Jane Austen's *Northanger Abbey*.[2]

The Gothic has been evident in Atwood's writing from the beginning of her career. The first poem of *The Circle Game*, "This is a Photograph of Me," asks us to look beneath the surface of both the charming snapshot and the lake at something less visible but more significant – the "drowned" narrator. Is she metaphorically "drowned" – denied, suppressed, repressed? Is she herself a metaphor for the natural forces which the circle gamesters seek to obliterate? Like many Gothic novels before it, the poem leaves us guessing at a mystery.

The Gothic contrast between innocence and evil, between pastoral and demonic views of the world, are repeatedly embodied in Atwood's use of 'innocent' matter-of-fact language to speak of ominous scenes. Like the peaceful seascape at the opening of *Jaws*, the language heightens the shock of the abruptly surfacing evil.

The explorers will come
in several minutes

....

they will be jubilant

....

but they will be surprised

(they won't be able to tell how long
we were cast away, or why,
or, from the gnawed bones,
which was the survivor)

at the two skeletons.

("The Explorers," CG 67)

In "Game After Supper" the pastoral setting of an old farm from "before" electricity becomes a scene of mildew and decay with "sagging porch" and an orchard "gone bad." The child's game is played with "two dead cousins" and consists of hiding from a man who will be their uncle only, the speaker tells us, "if we are lucky." As in "This is a Photograph of Me," Atwood leaves many details mysterious. Does the narrator play with cousins who are soon to die (i.e. is the term "two dead cousins" applied by the narrator retrospectively?) or play among the graves of cousins whom she is fantasizing into life? Is the threat of the "tall man ... coming to find us" an actual one or merely part of the child's game? To answer such questions would be, of course, to sort out the very issues of good and evil which the poem, and most of Atwood's other work, asserts are unsortable.

While such poems clearly seek to establish the 'naturalness' of fear, disorder, and death within the placid and the everyday, many others openly identify nature as the disruptive or 'evil' force. The conflict which Atwood is engaging here would appear to be the ancient one between man and nature that began ten centuries ago with Christianity's attempts to suppress the pagan nature religions.[3] The old gods of nature, particularly Pan, were identified by the Church with Satan and driven 'underground.' But as the psychologist James Hillman suggests, Pan can be driven only temporarily underground.

... Pan still lives, and not merely in the literary imagination. He lives in the repressed which returns, in the psychopathologies of instinct which assert themselves ... primarily in the nightmare and its associated erotic, demonic, and panic qualities.[4]

It is such repressed gods that that the woman hunted as a witch in "Harvest" (*I* 70-71), with her "potions," "mirror" and "crescent moon," is linked to. It is these gods that the narrator of *Surfacing* feels as a "power" during her breakdown in Chapter 23. A similar natural force is "the unnamed whale" of "Progressive Insanities of a Pioneer." As is usual in both the Gothic and Atwood, the force comes from underground, from "the swamp's clamourings and outbursts / of rock"(*AC* 37). The pioneer who attempts to repress this force with fences and furrows, is "disgusted" with it and calls it "an absence of order." Like Narcissus, he wants nature to mirror back his own image. His struggle becomes a parable not only for the unnecessary conflict between man and nature but for the Freudian struggle between superego and id, and the Christian one between dogma and natural energy.

It is important to note that Atwood frequently makes comic as well as serious uses of the Gothic image. Many of her characters are in love with such images, and would rather be heroes and heroines in a Gothic romance than live their own lives. The Gothic fantasy of "immortal" splendour rules the life of the man of *Power Politics*.

In restaurants we argue
over ...

... whether or not I will make you immortal.

At the moment only I
can do it and so

I raise the magic fork
over the plate of beef fried rice

and plunge it into your heart.
There is a faint pop, a sizzle

and through your own split head
you rise up glowing;

the ceiling opens
a voice sings Love Is A Many

Splendoured Thing
you hang suspended above the city

in blue tights and a red cape,
your eyes flashing in unison.

It brings to life "the billboard lady / with her white enamel / teeth and
red / enamel claws. "

the men
when they pass her
never guess they have brought her
to life, or that her
body's made of cardboard, or in her
veins flow the drained
blood of their desire.
("On The Streets, Love," CG 29)

In the story "The Grave of the Famous Poet," each time the man feels
weak or threatened he angrily strikes the pose of a hero.

He holds his elbows, wrapped in his clothes as though in a cape, the storm
breaks, his cape billows, thick leather boots sprout up his legs, a sword
springs to attention in his hand. He throws his head back, courage, he'll meet
them alone. Flash of lightning. Onward. (DG 91)

His woman companion who narrates the story similarly imagines
him a Gothic 'Count Dracula' villain whenever a conflict breaks out
between them – as here, where his comment about the castle gives
her a flash of insight into his tendency to try to 'own' her.

'I'd like to have a castle like that,' he says. When he admires something he
wants to own it. For an instant I pretend he does have the castle, he's always
been here, he has a coffin hidden in the crypt, if I'm not careful I'll be trapped
and have to stay with him forever. (83-84)

Most of the humour of Lady Oracle is similarly based on Joan's
longings to participate in the melodramatic and exaggerated passions and plots of Gothic romance. As a child, Joan listened to the
opera with her father.

As he never said much of anything, I would pretend his voice was the voice of
Milton Cross, kindly and informed, describing the singers' costumes and the
passionate, tragic and preposterous events in which they were involved.

There he would be, puffing away on the pipe he took up after he quit
cigarettes, poking at his houseplants and conversing to me about lovers
being stabbed or abandoned or betrayed, about jealousy and madness,
about unending love triumphing over the grave; and then those chilling
voices would drift into the room, raising the hair on the back of my neck, as if
he had evoked them. He was a conjuror of spirits, a shaman....
(LO 76)

As an adult she tries to have the best of both the everyday and the fantastic.

There were two kinds of love, I told myself; Arthur was terrific for one kind,
but why demand all things of one man? I'd given up expecting him to be a
cloaked, sinuous and faintly menacing stranger.... I kept Arthur in our apartment and the strangers in their castles and mansions, where they belonged.
(216)

Unfortunately for her peace of mind, she keeps mistaking the everyday for the fantastic – mistaking the Royal Porcupine in his "long
black coat and spats ... carrying a gold-headed cane, a pair of white
gloves, and a top hat embroidered with porcupine quills"(239) for
something other than Chuck Brewer with "the chin of a junior
accountant"(271); mistaking the ineffectual blackmailer Fraser
Buchanan for a roomful of "knife-wielding rapists, their fangs drip-
ping blood ... burglars, dope-crazed and lethal ... perverts who
would chop me into pieces"(284).
    As amusing as Joan's fantasy life is, however, it has an intensely
serious side. For like all "underground" Gothic images in Atwood,
Joan's fantasies carry vital information. Within the images of her
fantasies and the Costume Gothic novels which she writes from these
fantasies lie the keys to Joan's understanding of the person she is and
of how she was formed. By attending to these images, she can gradually understand her past and gain release from its control. The three-
headed monster of Joan's early dreams of her mother(66-67), who
eventually in Joan's poetry turns into Robert Graves' Triple Goddess,[5] "one in three"(226), reveals itself finally as three tired versions
of herself(341). The duplicitous men who have seemed both friendly
and rapacious turn out to be versions of any man she has known, the
helpless Lady of Shalott figure of Joan's poem "standing in the prow
... voyaging under sky's arch" appears finally as Joan's mother,
whom Joan realizes she had tied to herself through her fantasies.

She had been the lady in the boat, the death barge, the tragic lady with
flowing hair and stricken eyes, the lady in the tower. She couldn't stand the
view from her window, life was her curse. How could I renounce her. She
needed her freedom also ... (330).

Similarly, the Gothic image of "Progressive Insanities" carried
instructive "aphorisms" which could have saved the pioneer had he
listened; the church "swaying ... on its boggy foundations" could
have warned the cameraman of his "dissolving" photos.

## Refugees and Tourists
I was the one who didn't know the local customs, like a person from another
culture. (S 72)

Like Alice in Lewis Carroll's *Through the Looking Glass,* Atwood's
people stand before their mirrors, or wander in the confusing 'gothic'
world beyond the mirror, unsure of who they are or what powers
and size they possess. Some see themselves as small and weak, like
Susanna Moodie in the Ontario wilderness; some as comically large,
like the lover in *Power Politics.* They can see themselves as double
(Moodie in "The Two Fires"), or even multiple (Joan Foster in the
climactic episode of *Lady Oracle*), as thwarted ("Progressive Insanities") or as "powerless" innocents (the narrator of *Surfacing*). Few
feel comfortable in the circumstances in which they find themselves.
Like Alice, they find the world alien to them, feel variously unacknowledged, unappreciated, unfulfilled, and often wistful for another
kind of existence.

Atwood's most frequent metaphor for these people is the 'refugee'
or 'tourist.' This is the metaphor she proposes in *The Circle Game*
for those who feel separate from both the mass culture and from the
older natural world this culture abuses. The poem is "Totems," in
which literal "tourists" come to the park to "pose for each other's
cameras" in front of "restored" totem poles, while the narrator and
her companion are "tourists of another kind," unable to participate
in either the superficial rituals of pictures and postcards or in the
deeper ones embodied by the Indian symbols. "There is nothing for
us to worship," she tells us; her landscape is

dead trees in the seared meadows
dead roots bleaching in the swamps.
(CG 60)

Such images of radical homelessness permeate *The Circle Game*. The speakers often are travelling ("Evening Train Station, Before Departure," "The Settlers," "Migration: C.P.R."), living in rented rooms ("The Circle Game"), or dying of isolation ("The Explorers"). They feel as if they are "always moving," living "on the edges," ("Evening Trainstation," *CG* 15-16), they see their surroundings as cryptic, indecipherable.

... each of the
few solid objects took some great
implication, hidden but
more sudden than a signpost
("Migration: C.P.R.," 53)

The men of the poems about 'love' relationships are unstable, lonely and restless; they have "transient hands" ("Letters toward and away," 72), they engage in "aimless journeyings" ("Against Still Life," 65). In the book's title poem both lovers are caught

in the monotony of wandering
from room to room, shifting
the place of our defences ... (44)

In *The Animals in that Country,* the rooming house image that dominates the short stories of *Dancing Girls* becomes evident. Here the "landlady" is "intrusive as the smells / that bulge in under my doorsill"; she invades even the tenant's unconscious and blocks her dreams of escape.

and when I dream images
of daring escapes through the snow
I find myself walking
always over a vast face
which is the land-
lady's, and wake up shouting.
("The Landlady," *AC* 15)

In "Roominghouse, Winter," the speaker again feels rootless, ephemeral.

In the room itself none
of the furniture is mine
....
Tomorrow, when you come to dinner
they will tell you I never lived here.(28)

Foreshadowing her critical book of 1972, Atwood describes her condition as an "exile" in which "survival / is the first necessity"(29). The literal tourists of "Totems," the members of the mass-culture which has no organic relationship to the landscape, are also present in this book to further alienate those who desire such a relationship. The reincarnation of Captain Cook discovers everywhere he goes

... historians, wearing
wreaths and fake teeth
belts; or in the desert, cairns
and tourists.(61)

The speaker in "At the Tourist Centre in Boston" finds that the travel posters have transformed her country into "arrangements of grinning tourists." Her home has become plasticized, "a cynical fiction, a lure / for export only."(18)

... a flat lake, some convenient rocks
where two children pose with a father
and the mother is cooking something
in immaculate slacks by a smokeless fire
her teeth white as detergent.(18)

The immigrant and the settler are specific kinds of tourists who in Atwood usually have extreme difficulty in feeling at home in the new landscape. The pioneer of "Progressive Insanities" is one of these. So too is the native Indian in "The Settlers," who experiences the land as water, and his nomadic life as having "drifted, picked by the sharks," or as having been "stranded / on a ridge of bedrock"(CG 79). The Journals of Susanna Moodie is entirely given to the experiences of a settler who comes to see herself as "a word / in a foreign language"(11), who feels

... surrounded, stormed, broken

in upon by branches, roots, tendrils(17),

whose very identity is so undermined by the new environment that when her husband returns from the field she

... can't think
what he will see
when he opens the door.(19)

Another tourist, Odysseus of "Circe / Mud Poems" in *You Are Happy,* is mocked by Circe for his rootlessness, his failure to take responsibility for the direction of his life. Like the man of *Power Politics,* he is rootless because he has let himself be limited by myth, by a refusal to 'own himself,' to disengage himself from his "story." "In the clutch of your story, your disease," Circe tells him, "You are helpless"(64).

All of the narrators of Atwood's fiction are rootless, homeless wanderers but – unlike Odysseus – usually feel deeply dissatisfied with their condition. Five of the fourteen stories of *Dancing Girls* are set in travel situations, two are set in rooming houses, one at a summer camp, another concerns a short-term teaching post in Edmonton, and yet another a woman's sobbing departure from home in the face of probable atomic war. "The Man from Mars" concerns a young woman's encounter with a man from "another culture" who is so "different" that it is hard to tell whether he is "insane or not"(32), a man who, like a strange new land, makes the narrator feel disoriented and helpless. In "Under Glass," the lovers live in rooms on opposite sides of the city with the man apathetically receiving the narrator's visits. They seem no more than tourists in each other's lives.

A rented set of rooms is the setting for much of the action of *The Edible Woman,* with a landlady who "answers the front door for ... visitors before they ring the bell"(14). Marian spends much of the novel travelling between the rooming house, her fiancé Peter's apartment, Duncan's apartment, Clara's house, and her office, none of which she feels to be other than foreign territory. The opening set in *Life Before Man* is a marital home in which neither Nate nor Elizabeth feel comfortable. Much of the book concerns Elizabeth's attempts to claim her house and Nate to set up a new house with Lesje.

In this novel all three major characters tend to feel that their lives are "refugee" experiences. Lesje is surprised to find that Nate "expects her to be serene, a refuge, he expects her to be kind"(267). Her own sense of herself is that "she isn't like that at all," but rather that she is a "tourist or refugee" hunched under a fern watching dinosaurs in a Jurassic forest(19). Nate's wife Elizabeth looks back on her traumatic childhood and terms herself also "a refugee, with a refugee's desperate habits"(150). Like a refugee, she has married

Nate for "safety, relief: at last she was out of danger"(262). Sitting in her own living room she feels "as if waiting for a plane"(23); when she looks at one of the children's paintings, it appears to her to be "a foreign country"(37). Her vision of the children who come trick-or-treating on Hallowe'en to her door could well apply to most of the characters of Atwood's novels and short stories – "all souls ... come back, crying at the door, hungry, mourning their lost lives"(53).

*

... you see me not as human
but as cavern:
larval darkness and velvet shelter,
a rural motif, like a cow-fleshed
pumpkin,...
....
Is it my body or your vision
which is martian?
("Three Denizen Songs," *I* 66)

It is women as a group who are the lost souls in Atwood's most recent books of poetry. Mutilated in "Notes Toward a Poem that Can Never Be Written" (*TS* 67), circumcised, prostituted, raped and aborted in "A Women's Issue," (*TS* 54-55), fearing murder in "Him" (*MD* 56), imprisoned and totally "broken" in "Letter from the House of Questions" (*I* 76-77), experiencing themselves as Martian in "Three Denizen Songs," attempting to placate the archetypal male sadist in "Singing to Genghis Khan" (*I* 68-69), awaiting burning at the stake in "Harvest" (*I* 70-71), these Atwood women are dimly perceived generic figures, less individuals than symbols of common humanity brutalized by instrumental language and rationalist phallic technology. This dehistoricizing paradoxically creates what to the semioticist would be the very thing Atwood opposes here: an instrumental and generalizing second-order language. The women in the poems have been emptied by Atwood of their history and specificity, and become 'mythologized' representatives of abuse and oppression. On the other hand, the lack of specific characterization and the overt disregard for historical accuracy have the positive and practical literary effect of inviting the reader to see these women and their oppressors as contemporaneous with the reading process.

In the plum-coloured tent in the evening
a young woman is playing a lute
an anachronism
and singing to Genghis Khan.

It is her job. It is her intention
to make him feel better.
Then maybe she can get some sleep
and will not be murdered.

("Singing to Genghis Khan")

The poem thus refers a reader not to the historical Genghis Khan and his women but to all men in general as potential Genghis Khans, and to all women as potential slave-girls and refugees.

## Underground, Underwater

I myself was underground, I had dug myself a private burrow. (*EW* 76)

Where do refugees go? Physically they indeed end up in the transient accommodations – hotel rooms, rooming houses, apartments – of Atwood's fiction; spiritually or psychologically, they go to more distant places. "Underground" in Atwood's writing is the term that summarizes all the various escapes that the "refugee" can make from alienating rationalism. Sometimes, as in the case of Sarah in the story "The Resplendent Quetzal," or in that of Joan in *Lady Oracle*, the character buries what she is 'really like' in order to protect a relationship.

( ... if he'd known what I was really like, would he have still loved me?) The trouble was that I wanted to maintain his illusions for him intact, and it was easy to do ... I simply never told him anything important. .... In my experience, honesty and expressing your feelings could lead only to one thing. Disaster. (*LO* 36-37)

The 'buried' life here is often characterized by the kind of fantasizing noted earlier in the discussion of Atwood's Gothic imagery. Sometimes the character withdraws in order to protect both herself and another from the unpredictabilities of emotion. The narrator of *Power Politics* sends her feelings 'underground' because her lover prefers a superficial person ("I can't tell you my name / you don't believe I have one," [54]) and because she herself enjoys the games of assumed personae, her face

dissolving and re-forming so quickly
I seem only to flicker. (20)

In all of these instances both the unpredictabilities concealed and
the withdrawal itself become part of the irrational 'female' world.
The 'female' is not necessarily 'underground'; but in a culture where
'male' rationalism has attempted to repress all of life's protean and
irrational elements, these elements become themselves refugees,
become 'underground' by default. The subterranean world of geo-
logical and botanical process becomes the only refuge of those who,
like the narrator of *Surfacing*, find their own sense of holistic human
life rejected by a pragmatic, technological society.

In *Procedures for Underground* Atwood offers a variety of uses
for the 'under' image – to symbolize repression, the personal unconscious, the classical underworld, as well as the fertile natural world.
In the poems "Frame," "Midwinter, Presolstice," and "We Don't
Like Reminders," 'under' denotes the kind of psychological repression that Sarah practices in "The Resplendent Quetzal." The narrator of "We Don't Like Reminders," ostensibly trapped in a failing
marriage, imagines herself buried alive in a flower-marked grave.

The cut chrysanthemums sit
on top of my head in a streaked
milk bottle; I hear feet,
someone clipping the grass. (*PU* 22)

In "Delayed Message" this narrator imagines her other self (wearing
the same "grey / skirt and purple sweater") rising like an eyeless
spirit from the lake to confront her(19). Here underground stands
for repression and spiritual death. It may be the realm of essential
process – of "leaves sweating" and of "violent green"(*S* 179) – but it
is also a place where a human cannot permanently live. It is
dangerous because it is indifferent to human need; as *Surfacing*'s
narrator sees in the last words of that book, "the trees surround ...
asking and giving nothing"(192).

Several poems – "Creatures of the Zodiac," "Midwinter, Presolstice," "Dream: Bluejay or Archeopteryx," and "A Dialogue" –
show the underground to be also the personal unconscious, accessi-
ble in dreams.

In the daytime I am brave,
....
I have everything under control

But at night the constellations
emerge; ...
... their teeth
grow longer for being starved
("The Creatures of the Zodiac," *PU* (29)

Underground here is natural form ("constellation") rather than human "control"; much like Freudian psychology argues about the power of repressed experience, this underground's "teeth" grow larger for being "starved" or ignored. Again there is a sense of danger. In particular, the dream world is dangerous because it is unacknowledged by the waking life, not included within it.

The dreams are not so much alternate realities as messages from 'female' underground. They tell of estrangement between sisters, of a woman's struggle to deny unconscious nature's "reeds and lily-pads" by affirming the conscious self's "geometric flowers" ("A Dialogue," 12-13). The dream of "Dream: Bluejay or Archeopteryx" contains within it a further underground / surface division – a lake that mirrors the dreamer and the berry bushes beside her but reflects the bluejay above her as a

... man
surfacing, his body sheathed
in feathers, his teeth
glistening like nails, fierce god
head crested with blue flame. (9)

This message is of the extraordinary natural power veiled in the surface appearance of things. The mirror, as in *The Edible Woman* and *Lady Oracle,* is not a reflector of appearances but a gateway to hidden meaning. Underwater, like the water that claims Susanna Moodie's son ("Death of a Young Son by Drowning," *JSM* 94) is a mythic and instructive realm. Going underwater in Atwood's writing usually means entering an instructive, ominous, and potentially transforming experience, as the narrator's plunge into the lake in *Surfacing,* or on a comic level, Joan Foster's mock-suicide in Lake Ontario, Joan's character Felicia's drowning in "Stalked by Love," or Marian MacAlpin's baths in *The Edible Woman* in which she slowly gains insight into Peter's wish to sanitize her. Being underwater invariably suggests that the narrator is herself searching her personal unconscious for repressed insights.

"Two Gardens"(16-17) introduces the powerfully fertile underground garden of natural force that underlies all "measured" manmade gardens. In contrast to the cultivated "asters / the colours of chintz; thick pot-shaped marigolds" (the "chintz" and "pot" metaphors emphasize the flowers' manufactured aspect) are the mysterious "plants that grow / without sunlight," that "have their roots in another land." "Fishing for Eel Totems"(68-69) provides the underwater version of this theme. Here the narrator, while fishing, fantasizes that the fish she has caught is a "martian," a being from another reality. Again this creature carries news of another more fertile and more elemental 'land'; from it the narrator learns of the wordless 'female' language whose existence is implied throughout Atwood's work.

... that the earliest language
was not our syntax of chained pebbles

but liquid, made
by the first tribes, the fish
people (69).

This underworld of fertile energy is the "deluge," the "surf of undergrowth" in which the pioneer of "Progressive Insanities" stamps his foot and sinks. It is the "bush garden" of the *Journals of Susanna Moodie* which will "come up blood," and from which the wild strawberries come "surging" like ocean waves (34), the bush garden that tugs at Susanna's skirt with its "fingers" of "spreading briars"(41). As "Fishing for Eel Totems" tells us, the power of this underworld extends not only beneath the present reality but back in time from it. It is archaeological and zoological, passed on in the "caves of the earth"

as fossil skulls
of the bear, spearheads, bowls and
folded skeletons arranged
in natural patterns, waiting
for the patient searcher to find them
("For Archaeologists," *PU* 72)

Its forms are "deep under" – cave drawings "made with blood, with coloured / dirt, with smoke." Clearly they are also the petroglyphs searched for in *Surfacing* by both the narrator and her father, the childhood drawings searched for also by the *Surfacing* narrator, and the dream memories of her grandmother's hands reclaimed by Rennie Wilford in *Bodily Harm*.

The title poem of *Procedures for Underground* also establishes underground as the underworld of classical mythology, the underworld which Odysseus, Aeneas, and Dante enter in search of greater ancestral and moral knowledge. The poem begins with underground as the familiar Atwood "mirror" image.

The country beneath
the earth has a green sun
and the rivers flow backwards.

The inhabitants of this world are "always hungry" – like the "starved" figures of "Creatures of the Zodiac." Gradually the inhabitants appear like the chained prisoners of Dante's Inferno.

... those from the underland

will be always with you, whispering their
complaints, beckoning you
back down

Like the spirits whom Aeneas encounters in Hades,

those who were once your friends
will be chained and dangerous.

Like the instructions which both Aeneas and Dante must follow to pass safely through Hades, there are underground "procedures" that are essential to a visitor's safety. For underground, the female realm of "tunnels, animal / burrows or the cave in the sea," is not a place to inhabit but one in which to "learn / wisdom and great power," to "descend and return [from] safely" (*PU* 24).

"Procedures for Underground" opens the gates to a dominant metaphor in Atwood of the hazardous journey to insight and self-knowledge – a descent to Hades, as in Marian's visit to the Royal Ontario Museum in *The Edible Woman,* Joan's trances and mock-suicide in *Lady Oracle,* and Rennie's imprisonment in *Bodily Harm.* They also take us to the entrance of the maze, a traditional symbol in literature for the mystery of the underworld and a recurrent one in Atwood for the unconscious self.

## The Maze

I see you fugitive, stumbling across the prairie,
lungs knotted by thirst, sunheat
nailing you down, all the things
after you that can be after you
with their clamps and poisoned mazes
(*PP* 43)

The man in *Power Politics* – like many in Atwood's work – Odysseus
("Circe / Mud Poems"), Peter (*The Edible Woman*), Arthur (*Lady
Oracle*), David (*Surfacing*), William (*Life Before Man*), Jake (*Bodily
Harm*), Orpheus (*Interlunar*) is committed to surfaces and resists
knowledge of the unconscious or primitive. His resistance
transforms the unconscious into his enemy, the "poisoned" maze.

Interestingly, the maze image, which is a major one in Atwood's
fiction, appears rarely in her poetry. Possibly this is because her
fiction is largely about personal growth and change, which requires a
descent into the 'maze' of the personal unconscious, while the poetry
is largely about being trapped in the 'circle games' of bad relationships. The most developed maze image in the poetry occurs in "A
Night in the Royal Ontario Museum"; this museum, we note, is an
important part of the setting for both *The Edible Woman* and *Life
Before Man,* and is given maze-like roles in both novels. "The
labyrinth holds me," the speaker says of the museum in "A Night in
the Royal Ontario Museum." More correctly, it transports her,
underground, through cafeteria, washrooms, Greece, Rome, and to
the "skeleton child" which is the termination of Marian MacAlpin's
journey in *The Edible Woman*; and further to the "fossil skulls" of
"The Archeologists"(*PU* 24-25).

... I am dragged to the mind's
deadend, the roar of the boneyard, I am lost
among the mastodons
and beyond: a fossil
skull ... (*AC* 21)

even to the primitive early syllables of "rocks and minerals," "the
stellar / fluorescent-lighted wastes of geology."

It is an unpleasant but truthful journey, similar in this respect to
the journeys through most of the mazes in Atwood's writing. What
we miss here is its effect on the speaker – has she been changed (or

perhaps only depressed?) by what she has seen? The next time we encounter the 'maze' of the museum, in *The Edible Woman,* we encounter not only the imagery of the poem but the reactions of the maze-visitor. Three times Marian MacAlpin enters the labyrinth or maze, twice – like Theseus accompanied by Ariadne, or Aeneas by the Sybil – guarded by her rabbit-like friend Duncan. On the other occasion, at Peter's party, she is transported there in an alcoholic vision. On the first visit, Duncan takes her up the "encircling space" of a "spiral staircase"(182-183), through "labyrinthine corridors and large halls"(186) to the Egyptian mummy-room, where she finds both the "pathetic" skeleton of a child mummified by desert sand and the skeletal thinness of Duncan who attempts to embrace her. At the center of this maze is victimhood, the embrace of death. On the second occasion, her intoxication gives her a sense of wandering through "corridors and rooms, long corridors, large rooms" (*EW* 243), the precise words used to describe the museum labyrinth. In a scene which foreshadows the maze of *Lady Oracle,* Marian finds in the first important room the pot-bellied image of her fiancé at age 45.

No, she thought, this has to be the wrong room. It can't be the last one. And now she could see there was another door, in the hedge at the other side of the garden. She walked across the lawn, passing behind the unmoving figure, which she could see now held a large cleaver in the other hand, pushed open the door and went through.(243)

Here she finds herself "chirping goodnight" to a file of boring guests. "She ran for the next door, yanked it open." In this room, the maze's centre, the last room where there are "no more doors," she again encounters the male figure of death, her fiancé with his camera "aimed" at her, "his mouth opened in a snarl of teeth" (243-244).

Marian's final encounter with a maze is with the Rosedale Valley clay quarry – "a huge roughly circular pit, with a spiral roadway cut round and around the sides"(262). The words "circular" and "spiral" tie the quarry to the "encircling" "spiral" stairway of the museum. As in the museum, Duncan is her guide. Marian arrives at the quarry just as her body is reaching the center of the maze of its hunger strike – having begun by rejecting only meat, then refusing cheese, eggs and vegetables, "the food circle had dwindled to a point, a black dot, closing everything outside"(257). Marian's guide Duncan calls the quarry "absolute zero," "as near as possible to nothing"(263).

Through the quarry Marian is again confronted with death and annihilation – with the passivity and barrenness of her life and with the futility of her body's self-destructive rebellion against food. At the center of the maze is death – "empty space"(262), a "black sky"(264), and an "empty pit"(265), as vacant as Marian's empty stomach. But in both Classical mythology and Atwood's fiction, the maze is ultimately a double symbol; it is the home of death, the Minotaur, and the gateway to new life. Like the "destructive element" into which Conrad's Marlow urges the hopeful swimmer to "immerse" himself, the maze can save as well as kill. The symbol of the quarry in *The Edible Woman* confronts Marian with the rock-bottom desperation of her life, with the absolute need, as Duncan advises her, "to think of your own way out"(264).

In this use of the labyrinth, Atwood is following both its earliest Mediterranean traditions and more modern associations. The historical mazes at Lake Moeris in Ancient Egypt, in Minoan Crete, and at the tomb of Posenna at Clusium, Italy, appear all to have been constructed to protect something – in the first two cases a religious mystery, in the latter a burial. This reveals their double nature – dangerous to intruders but instructive to those who can read their mysteries. In the legend of Theseus's successful penetration of the Minoan labyrinth, we again see the doubleness – the maze and the savage, death-dealing minotaur at its center are dangerous, yet its conquest will free Athens of the sacrifice of youths and maidens to the monster.

The underground construction of the historical labyrinths connects them to the numerous tombs and catacombs of later periods, and to the mythological underworld. In the eighteenth century the labyrinth was a popular feature of the geometrical garden. Louis XV had one constructed at Versailles; the Earl of Salisbury had one created at Theobald's Park, and William III built one of hedge-and-alley design at Hampton Court Palace. The center of such a maze usually contained a statue, a covered seat, or a fountain. Late in the eighteenth century, labyrinthine crypts, dungeons, and catacombs became a staple setting for the Gothic novel. In M.G. Lewis's *The Monk* and Horace Walpole's *The Castle of Otranto* networks of underground passages served ambiguously as both dangerous traps and welcome refuges from villainy. In Ann Radcliffe's *The Italian*, as well as in the Lewis and Walpole novels, the hero undertakes quests in the bowels of ancient churches, monasteries, convents, and fortresses.

The maze of Atwood's *Surfacing* is a natural wilderness version of the garden maze.

... forty miles from here there's another village, in between there's nothing but a tangled maze, low hills curving out of the water, bays branching in, peninsulas which turn into islands, islands, necks of land leading to other lakes. On a map or in an aerial photograph the water pattern radiates like a spider, but in a boat you can see only a small part of it, the part you're in.(31)

The narrator enters it, like the heroes of the Gothic novel, on a quest for someone lost, here the woman's father. The father's cabin, however, is only part way to the heart of the maze, so too his drowned body. Her real quest, we discover, is for her lost self, and begins in earnest when she flees the cabin and her companions, to hide half-naked in the dense bush beyond.

I go along near the trees, boat and arms one movement, amphibian; the water closes behind me, no track. The land bends and we bend with it, a narrowing and then a space and I'm safe, hidden in the shore maze. (167)

As we saw in Chapter IV, this maze is again both ominous (the lake did, after all, drown her father, and the bush will not sustain human life – "there isn't enough food"(189), and instructive. Through its agency she acquires compassion for others, new feelings of responsibility for her own life, and also completes her quest for her father by gaining a spiritual sense of him which transcends her encounter with his body in the lake.

*Surfacing*'s linking of the maze with the descent into underground passages – the narrator's dives into the lake – is further developed in *Lady Oracle*. Atwood has indicated that the maze in *Lady Oracle* is in conscious parallel to Aeneas's visit to Hades in Virgil's *Aeneid*.

In Gothic tales the maze is just a scare device. You have an old mansion with winding passages and a monster at the center.... But the maze I use is a descent into the underworld. There's a passage in Virgil's *Aeneid* which I found very useful, where Aeneas goes to the underworld to learn about his future. He's guided there by the Sibyl and he learns what he has to from his dead father, and then he returns home. It's a very ambiguous passage, and scholars have spent a lot of energy analyzing it.[6]

There is in fact no literal maze in Book VI of the *Aeneid*, although the underworld passages Aeneas follows there to the Elysian field are tortuous and labyrinthine. What Atwood appears to have done in *Lady Oracle* is to combine both the ancient underground maze of

Egypt and Crete and the eighteenth-century garden maze with Aeneas's underworld descent. Joan Foster's descent begins with her mock-suicide in Lake Ontario (with Marlene and Sam together filling the role of Charon the ferryman of the river Styx), her flight to Terremoto (literally 'moving earth'), and climaxes there as she writes her novel "Stalked by Love" and sends her characters Felicia and Charlotte into an ominous garden maze. Joan's sybil is variously Aunt Lou, who bequeaths her both money and a beautiful body, the spiritualist Leda Sprott, and her mother. The theme of descent to the underworld is reinforced throughout the novel by numerous other incidents – including Joan's being tied to a tree in a ravine, her attending a spiritualist chapel whose congregation attempts to contact "the other shore"(106), her entering the mirror while doing automatic writing and "going along a narrow passage that led downward" toward a "truth that was waiting," her walking with her husband through "a maze of Roman streets" to "descend into the Catacombs"(133).

While in the underworld, Aeneas is transformed from an individual adventurer, lover of Dido, into the public man whose identity will merge with that of both his descendants and the city they will found and govern. He can be said, in fact, to die an individual and be reborn, through his father Anchises' vision of reborn souls, as one who lives his life through society. Joan Foster similarly begins her descent in selfishness, concerned only with self preservation, with being "... carefree at last, the past [and friends and husband with it] discarded"(3). She emerges with a sense of personal responsibility – to Marlene and Sam ("the first thing is to get Marlene and Sam out of jail, I owe it to them" [344]) and to the newspaperman she has recently assaulted ("I couldn't just run off and leave him all alone in the hospital..." [344]).

There are no obvious mazes in *Life Before Man,* although Lesje's Mesozoic swamps possess implicit labyrinthine qualities. The Mesozoic constitutes an underworld, and Lesje's decision that it is "a place you can't go to anymore" (290) and to be a person who is the "cause" of events is a 'surfacing' from it. Similarly, Elizabeth's visit to the domed planetarium is a kind of visit to the underworld of gods, goddesses (Cassiopeia, Orion) and cosmic blackness. She emerges from it, however, confirmed in her pessimism rather than transformed from it.

The continuing presence of the Royal Ontario Museum, however, gives *Life Before Man* an implicit maze of lost purpose, meaningless accumulation, empty routine – like the "maze of ... legalities" (163) Elizabeth constructs around her life. The museum is the ultimate collection, the ultimate example of the rationalist attempt to sort, catalogue, and organize experience. Its vocabulary is that of the technology that seeks to replace the flesh, as Lesje's vocabulary of time-classifying terms – 'Pleistocene,' 'Jurassic' – replace conventional sexual stimulation for William. It is not surprising that in fantasies Lesje should seek to mitigate the museum's nightmare boneyard qualities by clothing the bones of the dinosaurs in polka-dotted flesh. Although the novel may lack explicit maze imagery, the lives of the three central characters are painfully labyrinthine. They circle back on old actions, move at best tentatively toward new passages, often feel lost in routine, self-doubt, and family inheritance.

An explicitly Virgilian maze reappears in *Bodily Harm*, in the corridors of 'Fort Industry,' at the heart of which is a very special structure.

He steers her down some steps to a stone corridor, where at least it's cooler. ...

Dr. Minnow opens the door at the end, and they're looking at a small, partly paved courtyard surrounded by a wall. The courtyard is overgrown with weeds; in a corner of it three large pigs are rooting.

In the other corner there's an odd structure, made of boards nailed not too carefully together. It has steps up to a platform, four supports but no walls, a couple of cross-beams. It's recent but dilapidated; Rennie thinks it's a child's playhouse which has been left unfinished and wonders what it's doing here.

'This is what the curious always like to see,' Dr. Minnow murmurs.

Now Rennie understands what she's been shown. It's a gallows. (129, 131)

In a cell overlooking this gallows Rennie much later will watch Lora being savagely beaten, will hesitate to 'touch' or help her, and will discover an unconscious memory of the childhood scene in which her hands, her ability to touch, were taken from her. Once again at the heart of the maze will lie both death and instruction. One lingers here at the peril of one's life, but like Aeneas can be transformed to social responsibility. Restored to the use of her hands by her unconscious recollection, Rennie can reach out to help Lora even though "she dislikes her," even though "they have nothing in common except they're in here" (271).

## Metamorphosis

>   ... our breathing sinking
> to green milleniums
> and       sluggish     in our blood
> all ancestors
> are warm fish moving (CG 63)

Most of Margaret Atwood's optimism that the world will continue to change and grow is based on the 'female' pre-articulate world of vegetation and primitive zoology. In *Surfacing* it is by seeing herself as "part of the landscape ... a tree, a deer skeleton, a rock" (187), by feeling her "blood swell out like sap" (185), that the narrator begins to acquire purpose and identity. In "The Progressive Insanities of a Pioneer," it is with its "aphorisms" of a "tree-sprout" that the land heals itself of the pioneer's fields, fences, and buildings (AC 36).

The plants have their roots underground, "have their roots / in another land" ("Two Gardens," *PU* 17), and come to the earth's surface like Atwood's reborn characters. Their flowers are "gifts" that reveal another life – "brilliant images the eyes / are said to see / just before drowning"("Chrysanthemums," *PU* 61). In recent poems Atwood has pronounced the earth to be a crucible of constantly reborn life, an

>   ... acid sea
> where flesh is etched from
> molten bone and re-forms.

This sea is identical with the life of each living form.

>   ... there is no *other*.
> ("Daybooks II,"*THP* 97)

Organic matter here has sacramental qualities; all planetary beings seem to be sibling organisms.

> Good bread has the salt taste
> of your hands after nine
> strokes of the axe, the salt
> taste of your mouth, it smells
> of its own small death, of the deaths
> before and after.

Lift these ashes
into your mouth, your blood;
to know what you devour
is to consecrate it,
almost. All bread must be broken
so it can be shared. Together
we eat the earth.

("All Bread," *THP* 109)

Here the underground world is contiguous with the surface; although humans cannot permanently dwell in it, its energy and nourishment must be admitted to their lives.

In terms of these 'earth' images, metamorphosis is natural growth. The insect-eating sundew plant in *Surfacing* "feeds on disintegrations" to produce "pure white flowers, "petals now, metamorphosis" (167), and teaches the narrator also to change.

Through the trees the sun glances; the swamp around me smoulders, energy of decay turning to growth, green fire. I remember the heron; by now it will be insects, frogs, fish, other herons. My body also changes, the creature in me [the fetus she imagines herself to carry], plant-animal, sends out filaments in me;.... (168)

Thus the meaning of the central image of *Lady Oracle*, the caterpillar metamorphosed to butterfly, is larger than its comic dimension as ballet-school costume or an evangelist's cliché. It is a growth image, which signals Joan's essential hope, however ridiculous her efforts, to feel at ease in a living world.

## Signposts / Totems

there are few totems that remain
living for us

("Totems," *CG* 60)

What the refugee, tourist, quester, or visitant to the 'female' underworld most needs are guideposts and passports – symbols which will direct her or him safely onward in a realm in which "the received language" is not spoken. Like the immigrants of "Migration, C.P.R." the quester is desperate for meaning, for some "tree" of knowledge.

(every dwarf tree portentous
with twisted wisdom, though
we knew no
apples grew there (*CG* 53)

Every object she encounters seems a potential symbol.

> ... each of the
> few solid objects had some great:
> implication, hidden, but
> more sudden than a signpost

Yet the precise meaning of the symbol, as the immigrant discovers on encountering the "iconic" Rocky Mountains, is often obscure.

> (tents
> in the desert? triangular
> ships? towers? breasts? (CG 53)

As in the case of the above trees and mountains, these totems usually are associated with natural force and often have emerged from under the ground. The "eel totems" of "Fishing for Eel Totems," that bring news of "the first tribes, the fish / people" (PU 69), come from underwater. The giant tortoises of "Elegy for the Giant Tortoises" have also come from underwater to become "relics of what we have destroyed, our holy and obsolete symbols" (AC 23). The mysterious presence of "A Voice" has come from "the other country" – presumably the same underworld or "Terremoto" to which Atwood's various mazes and mirrors provide an entry. This presence pervades all space, is both "a part of the grass" and part of the earth's atmosphere which is paradoxically "inside his head" (AC 58-59).

In the poetry the speaker usually appears to know, more than intuitively, the actual import of such symbols. Even Susanna Moodie "knows" the meaning of "the summer fire ... the [autumn] trees melting, returning / to their first red elements" (JSM 22) or of the Heraclitean "blizzard" (58) or "white blizzard" (23) that repeatedly appears in her eyes. In Atwood's fiction many of these guidepost symbols are at best unconsciously recognized. The moose in the "Moose Beer" of The Edible Woman, for example, is clearly an animal victim parallel to both the rabbits that Peter hunts and the "planned cow" that Marian's stomach refuses to eat; its use in the beer commercial tells us of how our culture will glamourize the butchery and devouring of animal flesh. Yet Marian herself is no more than uneasy about the symbol. The family of stuffed moose in the opening chapter of Surfacing, with its message of damaged family relationships, is similarly obscure to the narrator of that novel. In interview comments on the "squashed" animals collected by the Royal Porcupine in *Lady Oracle,* Atwood hints that all of these animals may be intended as symbols of what she believes to be Canadians' penchant for seeing themselves as victims.

Why in *Lady Oracle* is the con-create artist's form squashed animals. It's a direct reference to my own book of criticism as well as the whole tradition of Canadian animal stories.[7]

None of her narrators come to this perspective, although – most important for their growth within the novels – two of them do become conscious of their identification with such victims: Marian with the rabbits, the narrator of *Surfacing* with the slain heron ("they will ... hang me up by the feet from a tree...." [183]).

In a similar way Marian MacAlpin only gradually learns the symbolic dimension of Peter's guns, cameras, and hunting magazine that so disturbs her. She is certainly aware that the cake she bakes at the end of the novel is a symbol of how she believes Peter has seen her, but she sees no significance in her own eating of the cake. When Atwood herself was asked in interview if Marian were "asserting herself in the baking of the cake," Atwood replied, "I don't know – nobody's ever been able to figure that out."[8]

The more sophisticated narrator of *Surfacing* actively searches for signposts to her lost father – for "a prediction" from a missing barometer carved in the shape of a man and woman(24), "for footprints"(49), "a button, a cartridge, a discarded bit of paper"(50), for "proof ... of [his] sanity"(103), and for "guides" to her own childhood beginnings. On her way to dive into the lake to seek further clues regarding her father's disappearance, she speaks of his petroglyph drawings as if they were instructions for entering a "maze," or sacred objects that the quester takes with him for protection in the underworld.

... I had a talisman, my father had left me the guides, the man-animals and the maze of numbers. (149)

The man-animal recalls the half-bull, half-human minotaur at the centre of the Cretan labyrinth (as well as the stuffed moose at the beginning of the novel); the talisman recalls the string given Theseus by Ariadne for his guidance and safety. The narrator now is obviously aware of the iconic significance of objects, and actively seeks to interpret them.

The narrator of *Lady Oracle,* as the title implies, also actively seeks talismanic or oracular instruction. She not only attends to significant objects such as the arrow that sticks in her rump at the Sportsman's Show which she sees as "a message from the dead"(120), but takes up automatic writing because she becomes "convinced ... someone had a message for me" (221). But Joan is not adept at reading the unspoken female language of things. She fails to see the Triple-Goddess figure (the three-phase moon goddess Diana-Aphrodite-Persephone – youth-maturity-death – attributed to pre-Christian nature religions by Robert Graves in *The White Goddess*) when it appears to her in her mother's reflection in her "triple mirror"(66), in her dream that her mother has "three actual heads which rose ... on three actual necks," in her own triple vanity mirror before which she conducts her experiments in automatic writing and finally in the figure of the "dark lady," the "one in three"(226) of the poem which she consequently writes. She is also unaware of the import of the many other 'goddesses' that enter her life, from the "frizzy-haired plastic goddesses"(79) of dolls that she plays with as a child to the "cult figure" she becomes herself in the eyes of her lover The Royal Porcupine. Her reply to him ("'What were you expecting?' I said. Three buttocks. Nine tits" [244].) also implies the triple goddess, but without suggesting her recognition of it.

In *Life Before Man,* a novel that abounds with lost, searching refugees, there are conversely very few signposts – a fact undoubtedly connected to the failure of the characters to "move" or grow very much during the novel. One clear sign is the letter Lesje receives from a child in "May 30, 1978," inquiring about dinosaurs and the Mesozoic period. The letter is dishonest, "bent on shortcuts"(289), and angers Lesje. It brings to her mind the helplessness of the dying dinosaurs, and the unreality of a period she has so often visited in her fantasies.

The dinosaurs didn't know they were in the Mesozoic. They didn't intend to become extinct.... Perhaps she should write the teacher. *The Mesozoic isn't real. It's only a word for a place you can't go to any more because it isn't there.* (290)

Immediately after receiving the letter Lesje takes one of the first decisive actions of her life, discarding her birth control pills and resolving to ensure that Nate makes her pregnant. The child's letter has ostensibly directed her out of the Mesozoic, out of her escapist passivity, and toward taking charge of her life in a way impossible to the dinosaurs.

Less hopeful signposts exist for Elizabeth in this novel; they direct her not to positive action but to stoicism and resignation. When she visits the planetarium, for example, she sees the sky as a "black" dome, and an unnourishing breast,

The auditorium is a dome; it's like being inside a breast. Elizabeth knows it's supposed to represent the sky; nevertheless she feels a little stifled. (75)

At the end of the planetarium show of comets, meteors, showering stars, and black holes it is the blackness and negativity of the universe Elizabeth believes she has seen, a universe populated, like her thoughts, with negative particles – "not ... not ... nobody ... no ... no ... no...."

People do not become stars of any kind when they die. Comets do not really cause plagues. Really there is nobody in the sky. Really there is no round sphere of darkness, no black sun, no frozen silver man. (78)

Echoing this emptiness is another signpost object Elizabeth attends to at both the beginning and end of the novel. This is a hand-made porcelain bowl, "Kayo's bowl," one of a set of three that stand on her sideboard. To the reader they tend to suggest Elizabeth herself and her two daughters, and also Elizabeth, her sister and her mother. To Elizabeth they represent annihilation, nothingness, and the peacefulness annihilation might bring.

There's nothing in them. What could you possibly put into such bowls? Not flowers or letters. They were meant to hold something else, they were meant for offerings. Right now they hold their own space, they own beautifully shaped absence. (24-25)

Elizabeth hurls one of these bowls at her Aunt Muriel in angry recognition of someone centrally responsible for the unnourishing and empty life Elizabeth experienced as a child. At that moment she feels "victorious," "savage, she could eat a heart." Yet moments later she is "curled unmoving on the sofa" and rather than being delighted to have smashed a symbol of her "nothing" life, seems to mourn the symbol's loss.

Kayo's bowl, which can never be duplicated. A bowlful of nothing. (219)

In *Bodily Harm* Atwood returns to an idea from *Surfacing* that a significant object can speak with more accuracy than can conventional language. Throughout this novel such objects vie successfully with language in Rennie Wilford's consciousness. For her, conventional language has been rendered fraudulent by sloppy usage; she repeatedly sees the phenomenal world juxtaposing itself with language to expose the shallowness of its terms – 'support,' 'life crisis,' 'terminal'. Here she has 'made love' with her surgeon, Daniel.

He was ashamed of himself, which was the last thing she'd wanted. She felt like a vacation, Daniel's, one he thought he shouldn't have taken. She felt like a straw that had been clutched, she felt he'd been drowning. She felt raped.
　　This is what *terminal* means, she thought. Get used to it. (238)

Earlier, on leaving the hospital, she had phoned her friend Jocasta to ask "if they could have lunch."

She wanted some support. *Support* was what the women she knew said to each to her, which had once made Rennie think of stretch stockings for varicose veins. Firm support, for life crises or anything else you could mention. Once Rennie had not intended to have life crises and she did not feel in need of support. (163)

　　The most instructive object that Rennie encounters in this novel is the coiled rope which an intruder leaves on her bed.

There was a length of rope coiled neatly on the quilt. It wasn't any special kind of rope, there was nothing lurid about it. It was off-white and medium thick. It could have been a clothesline.
　　All I could think of was a game we used to play, Detective or Clue, something like that. You had to guess three things: Mr. Green, in the conservatory, with the pipewrench; Miss Plum, in the kitchen, with a knife. Only I couldn't remember whether the name in the envelope was supposed to be the murderer's or the victim's. *Miss Wilford, in the bedroom, with a rope.* (13-14)

It tells her of the human will to control events with tools, with instruments; it tells her that she was to be the event, the one to be tied up like the dead heron hung from a tree in *Surfacing* or the young Joan Bennett tied by her girlfriends, in a ravine, with a skipping rope. It recalls for the reader also how *Surfacing*'s narrator saw male instrumentality in Joe's smile after she had allowed him to make love to her.

He smiles ... and lowers his face to kiss me. He still doesn't understand, he thinks he has won, act of his flesh a rope noosed around my neck, leash, he will lead me back to the city and tie me to fences, doorknobs. (163)

Rennie senses the full import of the rope left on her bed only when she discovers it again in the gallows yard of Fort Industry. Here it serves as the chief secret at the heart of the maze, the message that the rope is male, and that men use it to maim, and murder.

The man falls forward, he's kept from hitting the pavement by the ropes that link him to the other men, one of the policemen jams the cattle prod in between his legs, he's flung back, now it's a scream. Not human.

"She's afraid of men and its simple, it's rational," Rennie thinks. "She's seen the man with the rope...." The man with the rope here becomes all men, Daniel with his surgical knife, Paul with his 'small machine gun,' Jake holding her wrists together, "biting her neck." All her life Rennie has been unknowingly a target for the male rapist-killer. "She is not exempt," she realizes. Given the chaotic male violence spoken of by the rope, "Nobody is exempt from anything" (289-290).

# CHAPTER SEVEN

## The Short Stories

### 1. Iconic Prose

ATWOOD's short fiction contains some of her most successful prose outside *Life Before Man* and the prose poems of *Murder in the Dark*. For Atwood, the short story always has the iconic potential of poetry – to be oblique and enigmatic, to be a language structure of intrinsic attraction rather than one dependent on the action it narrates. It has the potential, in short, to act in the implicit way of 'female' language rather than in the explicit way of the male.

The brevity of the short story makes it a difficult form in which to tell a 'complete' story such as that of a character who undergoes instructive change. Unlike Atwood's four comic novels, most of her stories end inconclusively, with the characters gaining not changed lives but, at best, increased self-knowledge. The narrator of "Under Glass" gains strengthened awareness of her neurotic attachment to the world of plants; Christine in "The Man from Mars" comes to see only the emptiness of her life. The brevity of the short story also makes it particularly suitable to the use of symbols. But while in Atwood's novels characters have an opportunity to consciously interpret these symbols, and to attempt to act upon the interpretations, in the briefer form the characters usually apprehend symbols intuitively, and absorb the intuitions almost passively. For many characters – Morrison in "Polarities" confronting the "barren tundra and blank northern rivers" of Alberta, Will in "Spring Song of the Frogs" hearing the frogs' "thin and ill" sound (*BE* 180), Yvonne in "The Sunrise" standing in the "chilly and thin" light of a Toronto dawn (*BE* 265), or Sarah in "The Resplendent Quetzal" standing by the Aztec well of Chichen Itza – the symbol they have glimpsed seems to declare a fateful summary of their lives; rather than leading them to action and decision, like the symbolism of *Surfacing* leads its main character, the symbolism moves them toward acquiescence and stoicism.

Throughout *Dancing Girls* and *Bluebeard's Egg*, symbolism dwarfs plot; central symbols like the chemical garden of "The Salt Garden," the blood-stained egg of "Bluebeard's Egg," the greenhouse of "Under Glass," the gothic crypt of "The Grave of the Famous Poet," resonate throughout the narrative; characters respond less to each other's actions than to the symbols which impinge upon them. In many of the stories of *Bluebeard's Egg*, Atwood further diminishes sequential narration by constructing the stories in short modules of discrete incident; the story grows by repetition and accumulation of image and symbol rather than by linear narration. The modules resemble the seemingly disconnected stanzas of her poetry; like these stanzas they could be arranged into other sequences without significantly changing the whole.

Some of the most powerful stories of *Bluebeard's Egg* – "Significant Moments in the Life of my Mother," "Bluebeard's Egg," "The Sunrise," "Unearthing Suite" – possess this oblique, discontinuous structure. None of these stories have a meaningful chain of narrative event; "Significant Moments" and "Unearthing Suite," the opening and closing stories of the collection, both portray their central characters by the juxtaposition of separate anecdotes and the foregrounding within these anecdotes of an identifiable pattern of recurrent symbolism. The characters in all four stories are the same at the end as at the beginning; they have been intensely illuminated for us, however, by Atwood's isolation of their characteristic actions – Sally's repeated trivialization of her own person in "Bluebeard's Egg," Yvonne's compulsively segmented life of routinized art and one-day friendships in "Sunrise."

## 2. Dancing Girls

The first information we receive in *Dancing Girls* is carried by its paradigmatic title – not girls who dance but *dancing girls*. These women are not silhouettes on beer glasses, or on the stages of cabarets and lounges. They are the other female performers, filling social roles they have stumbled into – housewife, journalist, young lady poet, botanist, Blake scholar.

\*

The emphasis of the stories of *Dancing Girls* falls on the gap between the usual and the unusual, between the superficial veneer of social behaviour which convention, gentility, and propriety provide, and that 'female' underworld of violence, obsession, and jealousy that rages below. The sudden revelation in the stories of the horrific beneath the normal is reminiscent of similar effects in Poe's short fiction, of the crypts that lurk beneath ostensibly 'normal' monastic buildings in Radcliffe's *The Italian*, and remind us of the extent to which Atwood has adapted the resources of traditional Gothic literature to her twentieth-century materials.

*

The opening story, "The War in the Bathroom," focusses on the paranoid schizophrenia of the elderly woman first-person narrator, who describes herself in the third-person throughout. She is rootless, like most of the characters in *Dancing Girls*, living in rooming houses and having little trust in any human being. She imagines her previous landlady "was glad to see her go"(1), and believes an elderly male roomer in her new house uses the bathroom adjacent to her room at precisely nine o'clock each morning because "he does not want her in the house"(7). The schizoid separation between her thinking first-person self and acting third-person self dramatizes the usual Atwood separation between unconscious motive and conscious act. This separation is symbolically reinforced in this story by the presence of an old woman roomer, "the woman with two voices," one "violent, almost hysterical," and the other "formless"(8) whom the narrator later discovers to be two women, an old woman and her nurse. These are clearly another version of herself, the hysterical and violent agent controlled by the first-person "nurse." Because within her own personality this "nurse" completely rationalizes the fantasies of the underground self, the woman can learn nothing of herself, even when her violence results in apparent disaster for the old man whom she locks from the bathroom at nine a.m.

*

Surface reality in "The Man from Mars" is represented by the point-of-view character's upper middle-class Toronto home and by her expectations of various social proprieties; the underground world is represented by the young man from Viet Nam, who inexplicably insinuates himself into Christine's life, deluges her with letters, follows her "at a distance, smiling his changeless smile" wherever she goes. Being liberal politically by family tradition (her family employs a black maid, she herself had once even condescended to represent Egypt in her highschool U.N. Club), she attempts to rationalize his behaviour as part of "his culture." Although she finds the man unattractive and annoying, she also finds his attentions awaken parts of her that she has forgotten. A "solid," athletic girl, she finds herself being "mysterious"(28) to other men.

In the bathtub she no longer imagined she was a dolphin; instead she imagined she was an elusive water-pixie, or sometimes, in moments of audacity, Marilyn Monroe. (29)

After she has made the sensible conscious decision to have the man apprehended by the police, and learned that he has also been doggedly pursuing a sixty-year old nun in Montreal, her "aura of mystery fades." She reverts to the very orderly 'dancing girl' life she had been raised for; "she graduated with mediocre grades and went into the Department of Health and Welfare; she did a good job ..." (36). Again, this character learns little of herself from this encounter with someone "from another culture." While her unconscious self remembers her tormenter as an id-figure who might break through the French doors of suppressed sexuality (she has "nightmares in which he was crashing through the French doors of her mother's house in his shabby jacket, carrying a packsack and a rifle and a huge bouquet of richly coloured flowers"), her conscious self escapes into "nineteenth century novels" and rationalizes him as "something nondescript, something in the background, like herself"(37).

*

Repeatedly in *Dancing Girls* the underground and surface worlds fail to meet and nourish each other. In "Polarities" this failure is dramatised in the relationship between two young Edmonton university teachers – Morrison, who is cautious, controlled, self-sufficient, and Louise, who becomes passionately attached to a vision of a communal society that creates a mystic "electromagnetic" circle against "civil war"(57). Together they are two poles of existence: Morrison practical and isolated, Louise visionary and gregarious. His self-sufficiency leaves his life "futile" and "barren"; her visionary delusions so disconnect her from the everyday that she cannot prevent herself being committed to a psychiatric hospital.

In the closing passage of the story, Morrison encounters one of Atwood's recurrent 'signpost' images. He has returned to the city zoo's wolf pen which he had earlier visited with Louise. Beside the pen are "an old couple, a man and woman in nearly identical grey coats" – human versions of the wolves. The woman answers his question "Are they timber wolves?" only with another – "You from around here?" – and looks away. Morrison "follows" her "fixed gaze," as if it were an oracular instruction.

... something was being told, something that had nothing to do with him, the thing you could learn only after the rest was finished with and discarded ... the old woman swelled, wavered, then seemed to disappear, and the land opened before him. It swept away to the north and he thought he could see the mountains, white-covered, their crests glittering in the falling sun, then forest upon forest, after that the barren tundra and the blank solid rivers, and beyond, so far that the endless night had already descended, the frozen sea. (64-65)

Before this moment the story had been dominated by the circle image of the man-made electromagnetic field which the increasingly unstable Louise had believed maintained life in their northern city; here Morrison in the wolf-woman's eyes at last sees the real underground Louise had subconsciously feared – "the barren tundra and the blank solid rivers ... endless night ... the frozen sea."

*

Another familiar Atwood image appears in "Under Glass" – the glass image of *Double Persephone*'s world of "glass" and "carven word." Here the title refers both to the claustrophobic relationship between the narrator and her non-committal lover and to the greenhouse in which the narrator works. Another schizoid character, she wavers between human society and that of the plants she tends. When the story opens she is on her way to her lover's flat. "Today," she tells us, "the greenhouse has no attraction. I walk on two legs, I wear clothes." Like Joan Foster, she has unrealistic Gothic fears about men, plus a fear of the underworld of violence and dream.

He's on the bed, asleep in a tangled net of blankets, on his back with his knees up. I'm always afraid to wake him: I remember the stories about men who kill in their sleep with their eyes open, thinking the woman is a burglar or an enemy soldier. You can't be convicted for it. I touch him on the leg and stand back, ready to run, but he wakes immediately and turns his head towards me.

Like Lesje Green, and like Louise in "Polarities," she tries to protect herself from change and uncertainty by creating a non-human fantasy world – in her case a world of near self-annihilation, silent, and "nowhere."

Soon I will be there; inside are the plants that have taught themselves to look like stones. I think of them; they grow silently, hiding in dry soil, minor events, little zeros, containing nothing but themselves; no food value, to the eye soothing and round, then suddenly nowhere. I wonder how long it takes, how they do it. (78)

*

Death attracts many of the characters in *Dancing Girls*. For all of them the dance is deadly, formal, ceremonial, the dance of "plants that have taught themselves to look like stones." Moribund relationships are the rule in these stories – "Polarities," "Under Glass," "The Resplendent Quetzal," "Lives of the Poets," "When it Happens," "Hair Jewellery," "The Grave of the Famous Poet"; in most cases these are relationships that have been continued even though they have effectively died some time ago. In "The Grave of the Famous Poet" it is death which motivates the characters, which brings the man on his pilgrimage to Dylan Thomas's grave ("dead people are more real to him than living ones" [85]) and which keeps the woman in an almost necrophiliac fascination with her own situation.

One of us should just get up from the bench, shake hands and leave ... it would sidestep the recriminations, the totalling up of scores, the reclaiming of possessions, your key, my book. But it won't be that way.... What keeps me is a passive curiosity, it's like an Elizabethan tragedy or a horror movie, I know which ones will be killed, but not how. (87)

This is the most visibly Gothic of the *Dancing Girls* stories. The man's imagination is captive of graves and ruined castles; the woman's of being "trapped" by him in "a coffin"(84), and of murder – "maybe I should kill him, that's a novel idea, how melodramatic..." (88).

*

Fantasies of being raped are imaginatively little different from fantasies of being the victim of a stylish murderer or of being that murderer oneself. For the 'dancing girl' rape is perhaps the ultimate in being asked to dance a pattern that has been externally determined. Many of the fantasies of the narrator of "Rape Fantasies" (who throughout the story addresses a man whom she has just picked up in a bar) and those of her office co-workers are cast in standard forms of popular romance. Greta's man with "black gloves," Chrissy's bath-tub visitor, and the narrator's "obliging" man who helps her find the plastic lemon with which she squirts him in the eye are versions of the simultaneously threatening and attractive Gothic hero. The narrator's variously inept rapists – one becomes suicidal after getting his zipper stuck, another has such a bad case of acne she sends him to a dermatologist, yet another such a bad cold she fixes him "a NeoCi-tran and scotch"(100) – all involve her in variations of the nurse romance. The narrator, however, does struggle somewhat to over-come the romance stereotypes. At the end of many of the fantasies, she insists, perhaps naively, on the essential humanity of even a rapist. "I mean they aren't all sex maniacs, the rest of the time they must lead a normal life. I figure they must enjoy watching the late show just like anybody else"(100). Her overall narrative, which she speaks as a kind of "conversation" to someone we must regard as a potential rapist, ends on a similarly plaintive and hopeful note.

... I think it would be better if you could get a conversation going. Like how could a fellow do that to a person he's just had a long conversation with, once you let them know you're human, you have a life too, I don't see how they could go ahead with it, right? I mean I know it happens but I just don't understand it, that's the part I really don't understand.

Significantly, her companion does not once enter into her lengthily offered "conversation."

                                    *

"Hair Jewellery" presents us with another woman who does not understand why a man in her life could cause her pain. As in the situation of the rather reckless narrator of "Rape Fantasies," part of the answer is the woman's own behaviour – her finding it "easier to love a daemon than a man," her believing "dolefulness and a sense of futility are ... irresistible to young women" (109). Like the narrators of both "Rape Fantasies" and "The Grave of the Famous Poet," this woman is victimized because of her attachment to death and death fantasies. Her lover seduces her with his "melancholy eyes, opaque as black marble, recondite as urns"; he coughs "like Roderick

Usher," and believes himself "doomed and restless as Dracula." The
implicit necrophilia of this attachment becomes apparent to her in
the central symbol of hair jewellery, the "*memento mori*" of
allegedly enduring love.

The hair jewellery consists of memorial brooches woven of the
hair of deceased relatives; through her ambiguously academic study
of them (she is visiting the museum at Salem, Connecticut, to do
research for a paper on Nathaniel Hawthorne) the narrator comes to
see that her fixation on her gloomy lover is as rewarding as the self-
inflicted griefs the brooches memorialize.

I knew whose hair was in the massive black and gold *memento mori* in the
second row of brooches, I knew who I had heard in the vacant hotel room to
the left of mine breathing almost inaudibly between the spasms of the radia-
tor. (115-116)

Her Gothic fantasies are played out against a background remarkable for its banality and seediness — ill-fitting bargain clothing, run-
down hotel rooms, a Salem where wind and construction noises
drown out all thought of graveyards and witches. The hair jewellery
symbol, like many similar symbols in Atwood fiction, makes a concealed reality concrete and visible to the narrator; it allows it to 'surface' from a mass of mundane detail that have hitherto disguised its
lethal power as something at worst tiresome and banal.

This narrator seems, however, to have no other options than the
Gothic pretence or the banality of materialistic concern. When she
leaves her lover, it is for an academic job, a "silver haircut," a "sup-
portive" husband, a "two-story colonial" house. When she wearies
of these, she imagines her lover imprisoned in her cellar, "standing
dirty and stuffed, like Jeremy Bentham in his glass case"(123-124).
As in "Polarities," the unconscious life remains disconnected from
the conscious life; fantasy or imagination undermine rather than
enrich the narrator's intellectual achievements.

*

Fantasy takes over the main character, the elderly farmwife Mrs.
Burridge, in the rather flawed story "When it Happens." Hers is a
paranoid fantasy, similar to that of the point-of-view character of "A
War in the Bathroom." In a period of strikes, shortages, famines,
lay-offs, price increases, and inflating land values, Mrs. Burridge,
who appears to live somewhat north of Toronto, begins to fear the

outbreak of war, to watch for "smoke coming up from the horizon ... off to the south" (127), and to fantasize about how she would deal with the resulting social breakdown. As in "War in the Bathroom," she focusses on the violence she expects in others, imagines herself forced to stoically abandon her treasured heirlooms and possessions by "hungry people ... young and tough" (134) and deliberately killing to protect herself from two ambiguously "smiling" strange men.

Clearly, if all humanity were driven during emergencies by such fantasies as those of Mrs. Burridge, these would no longer be fantasies but realistic fears. The problem with this story is that, unlike in "The War in the Bathroom," Atwood does not signal whether her character is justified or unjustified in her fears, whether the author expects more from humanity than what Mrs. Burridge promises, or whether the story is merely an *On the Beach* doomsday scenario. Read alone, it has the effect of the latter. Read in the context of Atwood's general concern with the dangers of paranoid and Gothic fantasy, however, it becomes another statement of *Lady Oracle*'s lesson that fantasy limits human potential, prevents communication, and creates potentially lethal distrust.

*

In Mrs. Burridge, murderousness born of paranoid fantasy lurks just below the surface of a seemingly gentle, stereotypically grey-haired farmlady who cans, freezes, and pickles. Conservatism – symbolized by Mrs. Burridge's preoccupation with the preservation of fruits, meats and vegetables – conceals raw and unacknowledged violence. This is a common occurrence in Atwood's stories: the bizarre, violent, and unsettling, often associated with repressed sexual desires, appears suddenly from beneath an ostensibly banal or conventional surface. Such violence is a part of Atwood's 'underground' imagery – kept hidden in the cellars of bourgeois houses in "Hair Jewellery," or bursting with sudden 'Martian' energy into the lives of conventional characters in "The Man from Mars." It is usually associated with characters who have either no sexual life, such as Christine or the old woman of "The War in the Bathroom," or are involved in unfulfilling, grudging relationships. Mrs. Burridge, we note, has become bored with her husband ("she doesn't even feel like teasing him about his spare tire any more though she does it all the same because he would miss it if she stopped" [126]), has lost faith in his strength, and fantasizes his death with cold-blooded resignation ("she supposes she ought to feel more emotional about it, but she is well-prepared, she has been saying goodbye to him silently for years" [134]).

Annette, the point-of-view character of "A Travel Piece," as a travel writer works professionally to suppress "danger" and "unpleasantness," and to maintain the illusion of a conventional, smoothly-running world. Her readers "did not want to hear about danger or even unpleasantness; it was as if they wanted to believe that there was somewhere left in the world where all was well, where unpleasant things did not happen"(139). Similarly in her marriage, her husband, an intern, insists that all be well. When Annette tries to share with him some of her uneasy feelings, he seems "hurt that she was not totally and altogether happy"(141) and gives her tranquilizers to preserve that illusion. Annette has a vision of the world as

... a giant screen, flat and with pictures painted on it to create the illusion of solidity. If you walked up to it and kicked it, it would tear and your foot would go right through, into another space which Annette could only visualize as darkness, as a night in which something she did not want to look at was hiding. (140)

Usually, of course, the foot comes through the screen from the other side, from the repressed underground 'night' forces like the "man from Mars." Here the "foot" is not Annette herself but the crash of the airplane on which she is flying, a crash which leaves her floating on the Caribbean with five other examples of average humanity. Annette's immediate response is to 'paper' the event with travel clichés – "For exploring the Caribbean, a round orange lifeboat strikes an unusual note. The vistas are charming ..." (147). But as no rescuers appear, she begins to believe "they have gone through the screen to the other side"(148). The requirements for survival are simple and primitive – food, water, sex, sanity, protection from the sun. They eat raw fish, she hears "furtive copulation" in the night, the young student drinks sea water and becomes violent and delirious. At the close of the story he must be dealt with, but should he be allowed overboard as he wishes, "wasted,"(152), or kept and killed for food? Even in entertaining these thoughts, her companions have become "Martians"(153) – not creatures from outer space but from that repressed, unintegrated underworld of unconscious savagery that no one on the raft has previously experienced.

*

Such a contrast between the superficial and the authentic, the conventional and the savage, is present in "The Resplendent Quetzal" both in the title image and the sacrificial Mayan well or cenote which the Canadian narrator and her husband visit. The well's primitiveness dwarfs the genteel "wishing well" which Sarah had expected.

She had imagined something smaller, more like a wishing well, but this was huge, and the water at the bottom wasn't clear at all. It was mud-brown; a few clumps of reeds were growing over to one side, and the trees at the top dangled their roots, or were they vines, down the limestone walls into the water. Sarah thought there might be some point to being a sacrificial victim if the well were nicer, but you would never get her to jump into a muddy hole like that. (154)

The explicit sexual connotations of the well – here enlarged by the guide's tossing of his cigarette into it – make Sarah, who tends to believe she has "forgot" men, unconsciously aware that she is sexually attractive.

The guide tossed his cigarette butt into the sacrificial well and turned to follow his flock. Sarah forgot about him immediately. She'd just felt something crawling up her leg, but when she looked nothing was there. She tucked the full skirt of her cotton dress in under her thighs and clamped it between her knees. (155)

Ultimately the well moves Sarah to psychological honesty with herself, bringing to her consciousness her repressed grief for her stillborn child, and moving her, even beyond her conscious understanding, to attempt to allay this grief. Stealing an out-of-scale figurine of the infant Christ from a crèche that decorates the hotel television set – "it was inconceivable to her that she had done such a thing, but there it was, she really had"(167) – she hurls it back into the womb-like cenote. Two signposts, statuette and cenote, have reminded the would-be tourist that she is not a tourist but a refugee, a refugee from grief and death, and have pointed her toward a symbolic act of atonement and self-honesty. The 'other world' of her child's conception and death "for which there was no explanation"(169) has become real for Sarah in the 'otherness' of a Mayan well.

Throughout this story the familiar superficial Atwood world is also visible – in the tourists' guidebooks, sun glasses, and kleenexes, the ill-matched plaster crèche set, the Fred Flintstone-shaped radio that plays a Canadian-authored U.S. popular song, a television set that plays "a re-run of *The Cisco Kid*." Spanish-America is clearly being reshaped into a bourgeois U.S. image. The 'underground' world is visible not only in the cenote but in the ruined pyramids, the carvings of the Mayan rain-god Chac-Mool, and in the fleas whose bites "swell-up" on the narrator's husband.

The marriage between Sarah and Edward is another of the passionless, mechanical relationships that afflict Atwood characters. Not only does Sarah hide her grief over her 'lost' child from Edward, but she is bored by his interest in bird-watching, annoyed by his insistent economizing, and wishes he would "conveniently" die – "It wasn't that she wished him dead, but she couldn't imagine any other way for him to disappear"(161). Edward in turn fantasizes about

... crashing out of the undergrowth like King Kong, picking Sarah up and hurling her over the edge, down into the sacrificial well. Anything to shatter that imperturbable expression, bland and pale and plump and smug.... (158)

Theirs is a surface relationship that engages the deeper unconscious areas of their psyches only in frustration and fictionalized violence. Edward's fantasy cries out against the impenetrable surface that Sarah shows to him, "that imperturbable expression," and sees himself as reverting from a careful, penny-counting tourist to a crashing "King Kong." His envisaging the well as the means of Sarah's death implicitly acknowledges its ancient and primitive power, invoking this power against what he sees as her "bland" exterior.

As an acknowledgement of the well's power, Edward's fantasy parallels Sarah's throwing of the plastic Christ-child into the well. Her 'sacrifice' is visibly a propitiation of natural 'underground' forces she has – "self-righteous"(158) and "concerned for appearances, always" – apparently offended. She had approached giving birth analytically, mathematically.

All the time she was pregnant, she'd taken meticulous care of herself, counting out the vitamin pills prescribed by the doctor and eating only what the books recommended. She had drunk four glasses of milk a day ... had done the exercises and gone to the classes. No one would be able to say she had not done the right things. (168)

After nature denied her the child, "she took the pill every day, without telling"(168).

Interestingly, although Edward has yearned to "shatter" her "imperturbable expression," when she does break through her reserve by means of the 'sacrifice' and weeps "soundlessly" beside the well, he is unhappy and fearful.

'This isn't like you,' Edward said, pleading, as if that was a final argument which would snap her out of it, bring back the old calm Sarah. (170)

Although a character may yearn for something deeper and more authentic than shallow tourism and meaningless marriage, it takes more courage than Edward seems to possess to face 'underground' passions that are unpredictable and turbulent as much as they are inspiring and enriching. As for Sarah, although momentarily shaken by her glimpse into the depths of her own unhappiness, she "smoothed her skirt once more ... then collected her purse and her collapsible umbrella," and resumed her functional relationship with Edward. "Did you find your bird?"(170) she asks. The bird is the quetzal, like the cenote a magic symbol of Mayan civilization and its direct, if often brutal, relationship to the forces of earth. It is the thing lost, simultaneously an unrepressed incarnation of Sarah herself and Edward's own sexual energies. We do not have to be told he has not found it.

*

Alienated from passion, alienated from the natural responses of their own bodies, characters like Sarah and Edward, Annette of "A Travel Piece," or Morrison of "Polarities," require extraordinary circumstance — Mayan wells, plane crashes, visions of humanoid wolves — to regain awareness of the underground from which they have banished themselves. Rob, the main character of "Training," is a young man who has always felt intimidated by his parents in attempting to meet their various expectations. He too dances to alien choreography. His surgeon father expects him to follow the male family traditions of medical school and recreational baseball. Although not interested in either, Rob tries both, finding himself nauseated at the sight of blood and prone to injury in baseball. His mother's favourite picture of him is "in his choir-boy surplice, taken the year before his voice had cracked"(178). His parents have chosen his summer job on which the story focusses — counselor at a camp for crippled children, a job that meets both his father's medical priorities and his mother's sentimental piety.

For Rob the camp with its babbling hydrocephalics, its spastics with their plastic feeding tubes, and its earthy and exhibitionistic teenage cripples, is as unsettling as a Caribbean plane-wreck. He has nightmares of "bodies, pieces of bodies, arms and legs and torsos, detached and floating in mid-air; or he would feel he couldn't move, couldn't breathe"(180), nightmares which reflect his own unconscious crippling by his family, his having been amputated from both his own body and his wishes. He is confused by the latent primitive energy in Jordan, the severely crippled girl he is given charge of – "like some small fierce animal captured in a metal net"(172), embarrassed by the male teenager's locker-room humour, made both angry and jealous by the casual sexual couplings of the other counselors. He yearns for some vestige of the primitive and spontaneous – perhaps some Gothic fancy – to appear on his "bland and freckled" face.

He would have preferred a scar, a patch over one eye, sunburned wrinkles, a fang. How untouched he looked, like the fat on uncooked bacon: nobody's fingerprints on him, no dirt, and he despised this purity. (192)

*

Ann of "Dancing Girls" is in many ways Rob's female counterpart. Continuing in graduate school because her father believes you should "finish what you start," envious of graceful women with beautiful long hair, and "circumspect" in her relationships with men, she has given up her dream of being an architect in order to study in the U.S. the more practical profession of "Urban Design." Further, "she intended to be so well-qualified, so armoured with qualifications, that no one back home would dare turn her down for the job she coveted." As the "armoured" metaphor suggests, Ann dislikes people. In the green areas she hopes to design "she could never visualize the people. Her green spaces were always empty"(217). For her, green is not an underground image of vitality, but one of repression. If she considers the inhabitants of her design projects, they often become children who "would turn her grass to mud, they'd nail things to her trees, their mangy dogs would shit on her ferns, they'd throw bottles and pop cans into her aqueduct"(220). Or they become abstracted, desexualized, like the "dancing girls" at the wild party a "vaguely Arabian" roomer at her rooming house throws, who become in her fantasies "sedate" pastoral figures:

... in long flowered robes and mauve scuffies, their auburn hair floating around their healthy pink faces, smiling their Dutch smiles, the dancing girls were sedately dancing.

This is Ann's image of her own life – a sedate dance to her father's music.

*

Despite all these portraits of marginal lives danced to inauthentic measures, *Dancing Girls* – like most of Atwood's fiction – ends somewhat optimistically. The concluding story, "Giving Birth," completes the birth imagery of "The Resplendent Quetzal" and shows at least one character able to manage the Freudian integration of underground and surface for which all the stories have indirectly called.

Atwood employs here a curious narrative structure in which the narrator several times interrupts the story to disclaim being the same person as the "Jeannie" of whose giving birth she speaks. These disclaimers work to stimulate the reader's curiosity about the relationship between the narrator and Jeannie. The narrator's later comment that her present life is "solid" – "No more of those washes of light, those shifts, nebulous fears, the impalpables Jeannie used to concern herself with"(231) – suggests strongly that Jeannie is an earlier version of the narrator, someone not yet transformed by childbirth.

Into the pregnant Jeannie's life comes a mystery woman, "another woman," visible only to her, who unlike Jeannie "did not choose to become pregnant"(234), who appears haggard and bloated, and who on the night Jeannie calmly enters the maternity ward enters also "screaming from pain"(236). This unhappy twin is the familiar mirror image that so many of Atwood's fictional characters such as Marian MacAlpin and Joan Foster encounter. She is a self-image, recognizable even to Jeannie as "not real in the usual sense"(235), an embodiment of all the "nebulous" Jeannie's unarticulated fears and misgivings about childbirth.

Although unable to foresee the exact role of this doppelgänger apparition, Jeannie does expect something remarkable or even "mystical" to issue from her maternity ward experience, and expresses this in the descent-to-the-underworld image we have encountered many times in Atwood's writing.

She deserves a vision, she deserves to be allowed to bring something back with her from the dark place into which she is now rapidly descending. (240)

One thing she does bring back is the narrator, the new, solid dark-haired "Jeannie" who, as an integration of both Jeannie and the alienated twin is the outcome of both the birth and the story. Jeannie's "hair slowly darkens, she ceases to be what she was and is replaced, gradually, by someone else"(245). Of the birth, the narrator declares, "it was to me, after all, that the birth was given, Jeannie gave it, I am the result"(244).

"Giving Birth" is the story that approaches most closely the structures of Atwood's novels. It is noticeably Freudian, describing an initial separation between self and its repressed other and the necessary 'cathartic' integration that the healthy individual requires. Its movement from discordant selves to the single solid self of the narrator parallels the movement toward greater integration of self image that constitutes the principal experiences of Lesje Green, Joan Foster, Rennie Wilford, and the narrators of The Edible Woman and Surfacing. The use of the underground descent image for the central healing event of Jeannie's life reiterates the healing underworld descent of Surfacing, the descent into the mirror of Lady Oracle, the descent into madness of The Edible Woman. While from a literary point of view the repetition of this structure suggests a narrow conception of literary form, its use here in the last story of Dancing Girls suggests a resolution of the issues of entrapment and alienation raised by the earlier stories. Recognition and acceptance of the underground self can lead to integration, transcendence, and authentic dance.

## 3. Bluebeard's Egg

This second collection of stories reiterates the idea in Dancing Girls of a gap between the acknowledged and the real, between the rational surface of events and the symbolic meanings which underlie them. This is the gap that is humorously implied in "Loulou; or, The Domestic Life of the Language," when the main character's poet friends become obsessed with an apparent disparity between her mundane name and the 'earth mother' role they have assigned to her.

"What gap," Loulou asked suspiciously. She knew her upper front teeth were a little wide apart and had been self-conscious about it when she was younger.

"The gap between the word and the thing signified," Phil said. His hand was on her breast, and he'd given an absent-minded squeeze, as if to illustrate what he meant. They were in bed at the time. Mostly Loulou doesn't like talking in bed. But she's not that fond of talking at other times, either. (BE 66)

Indeed there is a gap between the superficial and pretentious language of Loulou's poet-friends and the 'realities' of her experiences, but Phil's analysis here amusingly adds to the problem rather than relieving it. In terms of Atwood's work, Phil – an intellectual user of words – is very much on the wrong side of the gap; on the other side is Loulou – who is "not that fond of talking" at any time.

Most of the stories of *Bluebeard's Egg* involve characters isolated from one another by this 'language gap.' Most focus on characters to whom the chthonic secret language of things and symbols is more real than rational human speech – characters for whom the world speaks in scarlet birds, multiplying crystals, sunrises, star-shaped cookies, an indulged cat, or fainting spells. These characters are misunderstood by those around them who trust man-made order and language more than the female language of nature – like Loulou is misunderstood above, like Yvonne in "The Sunrise" is misunderstood by the conventional young couple from whom she rents her room, or like Alma in "The Salt Garden" is misunderstood by her estranged husband Mort, whose favorite word is *"arrange"*(*BE* 207).

The characters of *Bluebeard's Egg* are for the most part older than those of *Dancing Girls*. Most are middle-aged, have been involved in disappointing marriages or long-term relationships, possess minor accumulations of property, major ones of history. Yet the women find that they are still 'dancing girls,' still filling roles assigned to them by men. Sally in "Bluebeard's Egg" plays both devoted wife to her diffident husband and girl-Friday to her incompetent boss. Loulou may always have to play the uneducated earth mother. Like the two older sisters in the fable of the wizard's egg which Sally encounters in her "Forms of Narrative Fiction" class, most accept men's rules for life, or – like the youngest – give continued power to men's rules by pretending to follow them.

*

The central character of "Significant Moments in the Life of my Mother" is a woman who has accepted most of the rules she has been given for her life. She has played with these rules – hoodwinked her autocratic father into letting her have her hair cut, invented comic ways of maintaining propriety when afflicted with popped zippers or fallen underpants, devised a means to attend university despite her father's disapproval. But she has never perceived these rules as anything other than benign, or her transgressions as anything more than "fun". In consequence, she has become a good-humoured trivializer of life and death:

> "I remember the time we almost died," says my mother. Many of her stories begin this way. (*BE* 22)

She re-writes her family's history into charming but superficial stories of amusing misbehaviour, 'cute' idiosyncrasy. The language of these stories is the received one of cliché – "He could wind you around his little finger" (25), "There you sat, happy as a clam" (26), "You had something cooking." Not surprisingly, when the daughter who narrates the story matures and returns home with "modern poetry and histories of Nazi atrocities" (28) – material which resists sentimentalization – the mother appears distressed, looks at her as if "at any time I might open my mouth and out would come a language she had never heard before"(29).

Despite her various rebellions, the mother's language has remained that of the rule-giver; her view of all dissatisfaction with the status quo is that it can be overcome by exercise and cheerfulness – "There wasn't a lot that a brisk sprint through dead leaves, howling winds, or sleet couldn't cure"(28). The daughter's "creeping despondency" and angst make her seem to the mother, like the Vietnamese student seemed to the stolid Christine of "The Man from Mars," utterly alien.

> I had become a visitant from outer space, a time traveller come back from the future, bearing news of a great disaster. (29)

*

Throughout "Significant Moments" there is an impression – partly created by the modular structure, partly by the narrator's observations, partly by the different stories the mother tells to men and to women, and partly by the contrast between her comic narrative style and the non-comic quality of the events she narrates – that men and women inhabit separate worlds.

> Here my father looked modestly down at his plate. For him, there are two worlds: one containing ladies, in which you do not use certain expressions, and another one – consisting of logging camps and certain haunts of his youth, and of gatherings of acceptable sorts of men – in which you do. To let the men's world slip over verbally into the ladies' would reveal you as a

mannerless boor, but to carry the ladies' world over into the men's brands
you a prig and maybe even a pansy. This is the word for it. All this is well
understood between them.

.....

There are some stories which my mother does not tell when there are men
present .... These are stories of romantic betrayals, unwanted pregnancies,
illnesses of various horrible kinds, marital infidelities, mental breakdowns,
tragic suicides .... (21)

These women's stories are recognizably those of Gothic romance, in
which evil can be entertaining without being dangerous. Here too,
men and women occupy separate worlds – the men of power and
arrogance, the women of weakness and despair.

In "Hurricane Hazel" this separation of the sexes takes the form
of the young narrator's father being an "explorer for a logging company" and therefore absent much of the year, while her mother looks
after the family in a series of makeshift cabins. Similarly, the
narrator's brother is away in the summers as a "Junior Ranger, cutting brush by the sides of highways somewhere in northern Ontario"
(35), while she stays with her mother aspiring to have a boyfriend in
order to be "normal". In both stories the men define themselves by
their jobs or professions, while the women define themselves in terms
of their men, whose presence bestows 'normality.' This normality,
whether expressed in conventional marriages, cliché language, or in
high school dating customs, becomes for the stories' narrators the
'Bluebeard's egg' – the payment women accept to surrender their
selfhood. Normality, the ordinary, is dangerous, the narrator of
"Hurricane Hazel" concludes on the stormy night when she and her
gas-station attendant boyfriend break up because she has refused to
go out with him in ominous weather. The night is that in 1954 of
Toronto's Hurricane Hazel, and in the morning she looks at the
storm's deadly debris and is surprised by its banality. "This is what I
have remembered most clearly about Buddy: the ordinary looking
wreckage, the flatness of the water, the melancholy light"(59).

*

The title story of *Bluebeard's Egg* underscores these conventional
and unequal relationships between men and women. The main character is Sally, a woman who wants a conventional marriage, a conventionally beautiful house, and who has hired an interior decorator

to shape her house and married Ed, a "cute" heart surgeon who has "allure" to women, to serve as her husband. Like the mother of "Significant Moments," Sally habitually trivializes and jokes about things that she may truly care about – particularly her night school courses.

She was ... intending to belittle the course, just slightly. She always did this with her night school courses, so that Ed wouldn't get the idea that there was anything in her life that was even remotely as important as he is. But Ed didn't seem to need this amusement or this belittlement. He took her information earnestly, gravely. (155)

In fact, women are quite irrelevant, almost inter-changeable, to Ed, for whom Sally is his third wife. He is self-absorbed, absorbed in his profession, self-insulated from any emotional demands which might complicate his life. He listens to all women in the same ingenuous, grave, but unhearing way.

The wizard's egg fable, embedded into the story as material Sally has received in her fiction course, concerns a similar man – one to whom women are interchangeable. Three sisters are seized in turn by a wizard, taken to his house, and tested to determine their suitability to be his bride. The test entrusts them with an egg they must carry with them, and with custody of a room they are forbidden to enter. The first two enter the room, discover dismembered female bodies, let the egg fall into a basin of blood, and are found out, killed, and dismembered by the wizard. But the third puts the egg aside before opening the room; the wizard thus does not discover her disobedience and marries her. The three sisters correspond not only to the three wives of the heart surgeon and to the three wives of the psychiatrist Joseph in "The Sin Eater" but in a metaphoric way to all women in the collection who, like the mothers of "Significant Moments" and "Hurricane Hazel," have accepted the Bluebeard's egg of self-effacement and dependency in a traditional marriage.

*

All three of the above stories suggest that women accept the 'egg' of deferential existence ingenuously. They mistake the man by seeing him as powerful and glamourous; they mistake themselves by taking the role of custodian of his egg seriously. Such is also the case in "Betty," a story which is more about the growth of its young female narrator than about the title character. As a little girl, the narrator is

fascinated by Betty's womanizing salesman husband Fred, a fascination she also finds in the commercial shipping of the St. Mary's River
beside which she lives.

The freighters were huge, cumbersome, with rust staining the holes for their
anchor chains and enormous chimneys from which the smoke spurted in
grey burps. When they blew their horns, as they always did when approach-
ing the locks, the windows in our cottage rattled. For us, they were magical.
Sometimes things would drop or be thrown from them, and we would watch
these floating objects eagerly, running along the beach to be there when they
landed, wading out to fish them in. Usually these treasures turned out to be
only empty cardboard boxes or punctured oil cans, oozing dark brown
grease and good for nothing. Several times we got orange crates, which we
used as cupboards or stools in our hide-outs.

Structurally this passage shows the narrator in the same relationship
to the freighters as Betty is to Fred – living in the shadow of his
glamour, accepting cast-offs. As the narrator grows, however, her
interest turns to Betty. At first she tries to romanticize her into a
Gothic victim – "a stricken and martyred woman ... a woman who
had narrowly escaped death ... an aura of sacrificial blood surrounded her"(129-130). When Betty dies of a brain tumour, she sees
her as someone punished "for being devoted and obliging," who
died screaming "against the unfairness of life"(131). These images
show the narrator now trying to glamourize failure; like the Gothic
throughout Atwood's work, they serve to subjugate woman by making her fate as Bluebeard's wife seem interesting. The narrator's final
act, however, is to refuse both the gothic and her childhood impression that Fred was attractive and significant. It is Betty who is now
"mysterious".

Fred ... no longer intrigues me. The Freds of this world make themselves
explicit by what they do and choose. It is the Bettys who are mysterious.
(132)

In effect, the narrator has deconstructed the Bluebeard legend; Bluebeard is not powerful, he is ordinary; the mystery lies not in his dominance but in the woman's having naively granted it to him.

*

'In Wales,' he says, 'mostly in the rural areas, there was a personage known
as the Sin Eater. When someone was dying the Sin Eater would be sent for.
The people of the house would prepare a meal and place it on the coffin.

They would have the coffin all ready, of course: once they'd decided you were going off, you had scarcely any choice in the matter. According to other versions, the meal would be placed on the dead person's body, which must have made for some sloppy eating, one would have thought. In any case the Sin Eater would devour this meal and would also be given a sum of money. It was believed that all the sins the dying person had accumulated during his lifetime would be removed from him and transmitted to the Sin Eater. The Sin Eater thus became absolutely bloated with other people's sins. She'd accumulate such a heavy load of them that nobody wanted to have anything to do with her; a kind of syphilitic of the soul, you might say.' ("The Sin Eater," *BE* 231-232)

Soon after relating this, Joseph, the narrator's psychiatrist, dies and his wife and two ex-wives host a post-funeral reception at which they and his mostly female patients feed. Here are more images of the sub-servient female, patient to the man's doctoral wisdom, martyr to his need to be "free from sin"(241). The role deprives the woman of individuality; Joseph's three wives "have a family resemblance – they're all blondish and vague around the edges"(240).

"The Sin Eater" is narrated in a discontinuous first person narra-tive in which the discontinuity and the frequent telescoping of time suggests further the fragmentation of personality a woman's depen-dency on a man creates. The female language of symbolic image and dream informs the narrator's awareness but does not influence her conscious decisions. She dimly perceives a picture of blue "Krishna playing the flute, surrounded by adoring maidens" as having some-thing to do with herself and the death of Joseph, but can make no clear connection. At the story's close she is dreaming of eating Joseph's sins – in the shape of the moon and star cookies baked by his first wife – but as cosmic shapes in "dark space."

... this is not what I ordered, it's too much for me, I might get sick. Maybe I could send it back; but I know this isn't possible. (244)

And she reaches out to begin eating.

*

Four of the stories in *Bluebeard's Egg* – "Uglypuss," "Spring Song of the Frogs," "Scarlet Ibis," and "The Sunrise" – show characters in search of something more than what the inherited social patterns offer. But, like the narrator of "The Sin Eater," they have extreme difficulty in making their intuitions conscious. Their problem tends to be linguistic; there seems to be no words available to articulate what they feel or desire. In "Spring Song of the Frogs," Will, whether with his anorexic niece Cynthia, his narcissistic date Robyn, or his self-preoccupied lover Diana, "doesn't know what to say"(172). He frequently desires not to speak – not to ask Diana about her illness, not to risk telling Cynthia "You're pretty now"(174). The three women have withdrawn from inherited female roles, particularly Robyn and Cynthia, but have not found authentic creative selves. They have become shadows of traditional woman, crippled moons (both Diana and Cynthia, we note, were Roman moon-goddesses). At the close of the story Will and Diana stand under a "cold and lopsided moon". He finds her "angular, awkward," and though he "would like to kiss her" hesitates just as he has hesitated to speak before.

In "Uglypuss," Joel wanders from woman to woman looking for "someone to go home with ... in the hope that this unknown place, yet another unknown place, will finally contain something he wants to have" (95). But Joel cannot define 'home'. He too lacks language, possesses only clichés – "a golden oldie, a mansion that's seen better days"(83) he describes his rooming house as the story opens.

In two of these four stories the characters encounter a symbol which illuminates their lives yet which they are unable to make full use of because of their difficulties with language. Yvonne, in "The Sunrise," who writes jokes and pleasantries on filing cards so she will not fail in conversation, cannot fully seize even the sunrises she is so compulsively drawn to watch. The correct word escapes her.

And yet she knows that her dependence is not on something that can be grasped, held in the hand, kept, but only on an accident of language, because *sunrise* should not be a noun. The sunrise is not a thing, but only an effect of the light caused by the positions of two astronomical bodies in relation to each other. The sun does not really rise at all, it's the earth that turns. The sunrise is a fraud.

Thus too male-female relationships – clearly symbolized in the mating of the two planetary 'bodies,' are a fraud to Yvonne. The conjunction cannot be be either spoken or valued.

Christine in "Scarlet Ibis" (a story remarkably similar in its symbolism to "The Resplendent Quetzal" of *Dancing Girls*) successfully guides her unhappy husband and child to a view of birds so splendid that the "weight" of life lifts momentarily from her body.

Don took hold of Christine's hand, a thing he had not done for some time; but Christine, watching the birds, noticed this only afterwards. She felt she was looking at a picture, of exotic flowers or of red fruit growing on trees, evenly spaced, like the fruit in the gardens of mediaeval paintings, solid, clear-edged, in primary colours. On the other side of the fence was another world, not real but at the same time more real than the one on this side, the men and women in their flimsy clothes and aging bodies, the decrepit boat. Her own body seemed fragile and empty, like blown glass.

But when back in Canada she comes to retell the story, she lapses into formulaic humour, travelogue clichés.

She put in the rather hilarious trip back to the wharf, with the Indian standing up in the bow, beaming his heavy-duty flashlight at the endless, boring mangroves, and the two men in the baseball caps getting into a mickey and singing dirty songs.

She ended with the birds, which were worth every minute of it, she said. She presented them as a form of entertainment, like the Grand Canyon: something that really ought to be seen, if you liked birds, and if you should happen to be in that part of the world. (200-201)

Like the mother in "Significant Moments," Christine cannot face for long the primitive but authentic language of objects and events, but must trivialize it with banal humour and the superficial formulae of everyday speech.

*

*Bluebeard's Egg* ends not in optimism, as does *Dancing Girls,* but in benevolence. The concluding story, "Unearthing Suite," is narrated by a young woman who loves her parents despite being aware of the inequality of their relationship. She is particularly aware of the lack of privacy, the overwork, and emotional stress her independent-spirited mother has incurred by having allowed her husband, an "affable" entomologist, to give throughout their marriage a total commitment to his profession. The conclusion of the story emphasizes the different "languages" the mother and father speak – the father the male language of management and control, the mother a female one of intuition and poesis. They have discovered a fisher's droppings on the roof of their cabin.

For my father this dropping is an interesting biological phenomenon. He has noted it and filed it, along with all the other scraps of fascinating data he notes and files.

For my mother however, this is something else. For her this dropping –
this hand-long, two-fingers-thick, black, hairy dropping – not to put too fine
a point on it, this deposit of animal shit – is a miraculous token, a sign of
divine grace; as if their mundane, familiar, much-patched but at times still-
leaking roof has been visited and made momentarily radiant by an unknown
but by no means minor god.

The story returns to the 'language gap' of "Loulou," "Significant
Moments," and "Hurricane Hazel." We are still, despite the warmth
of the story, in the world of the wizard and his egg, where man
dissects, dismembers, "notes and files," and where woman 'pays a
price' to be both married and "cheerful." "What is my mother's
secret? ... What was the trade-off, what did she sign over to the Devil,
for this limpid tranquility?"(276) the daughter asks herself. The
price, she discovers, is innocence, not knowing.

"I don't know why not," said my mother. That is her secret. (278)

In this innocence she resembles "accepting, uncomplaining"(132)
Betty and Loulou – women who have never questioned the male
assumptions which surround their lives or seen consciously how different Bluebeard's analytical dismembering language is from their
own.

CHAPTER EIGHT

# *Survival*: The Victim Theme

MARGARET Atwood's most influential and controversial book is *Survival:* "A Thematic Guide to Canadian Literature," published in 1972. Even before the book was released, *The Toronto Star* reported its "staggering first printing of 20,000, with college-course outlines snapping it up sight unseen."[1] On publication, critical opinion was – with only a few reservations – overwhelmingly positive. The *Star* headlined its review by Robert Fulford "A Clever and Effective Analysis of the Literature of Canada,"[2] the *Globe and Mail* review by Phyllis Grosskurth pronounced *Survival* "the most important book that has come out of this country,"[3] *The Listener* declared it a "brilliant exploration of Canadian literature."[4] The reviewers' reservations were directed toward its style – "slightly better than slipshod" (Fraser Sutherland, *Books in Canada*),[5] its "wrong-headed" ignoring of both achievements in literary form and writing which contradicted its thesis (Gary Geddes, *The Malahat Review*),[6] its claiming for Canada of a "dominant theme in the literature of our time" (Morris Wolfe, *Saturday Night*).[7]

Nearly twelve years later it is evident that *Survival* itself, and the excitement created by it, were more manifestations of an intensely nationalistic period in Canadian history than permanent alterations to the national literature. The book provided a readable and witty access to Canadian literature at a time of great public desire for such access. It was openly sociological rather than literary in its approach, seeking to use the literature to define "a national habit of mind." *Survival* was also specific to Atwood's own writing and those of many of her fellow Ontario writers; as one reviewer remarked, it provided "an illuminating approach to the kinds of poetry and fiction that Margaret Atwood and many of her contemporaries are writing and are most interested in reading."[8] Much of the book's focus was not on Canadian literature generally but on writers published by House of Anansi, the publisher of *Survival*; 42% of the titles in Anansi's

1972 catalog were recommended by Atwood in *Survival*'s various
reading lists; the major Anansi writers of the time, Graeme Gibson,
Roch Carrier, and Dennis Lee, were among the four most recommended authors of the lists.

The difficulties, however, that *Survival* created for Canadian criticism were considerable. In its thematic approach – i.e. in selecting
texts for discussion on the basis of the ideas they contained rather
than on the basis of literary artistry – the book seemed to reaffirm
Northrop Frye's unfortunate remark that the evaluation of Canadian literature can be "only a huge debunking project."⁹ Although
Atwood claimed intermittently to be concerned with the quality and
form of literature as well as with its ideas, her emphasizing of Pratt
over Smith and Scott, Lee over Layton, and Gibson over Laurence
suggested strongly that she believed the explicit message of a work to
be more significant in determining literary 'tradition' than the implications of literary form. Certainly *Survival* appeared to stimulate the
writing of other thematic surveys – Elizabeth Waterston's *Survey*
(1973), Laurence Ricou's *Vertical Man, Horizontal World* (1973),
John Moss's *Patterns of Isolation* (1974) and *Sex and Violence in the
Canadian Novel* (1978).

*Survival* was also problematic in being one of many Canadian
attempts in the late 1960s and early 1970s to establish or 'fix' a
definition of Canadian culture. Similar to the Atwood work in this
regard were Al Purdy's *The New Romans* (1968), William
Kilbourn's *A Canadian Guide to the Peaceable Kingdom* (1970),
Frye's *The Bush Garden* (1971), Redekop's *The Star-Spangled
Beaver* (1971), and Fulford, Godfrey, and Rotstein's *Read Canadian*
(1972). The potential harm of these books lay in their creation of
overly narrow cultural definitions and restricted canons of national
writing. As Atwood herself remarked, there are "dangers of cliché
writing once there's a defined tradition" (*Su* 237). *Survival* created a
special problem here for Canadian criticism by taking a unitary,
Ontario-based centralist view of the literature. Atwood did not see
Canada and its literature through the differing perspectives of its
regions or the differing aesthetics of its writers, but attempted to
explain Canada through a single theory based on a single symbolic
image. This image was the wilderness of northern Ontario, which
became in *Survival* the 'Canadian' wilderness. The indifference and
potentially sinister natural force of this wilderness was the same as
that experienced by the narrator of *Surfacing* on the Quebec-Ontario
border near North Bay, or by Susanna Moodie in Ontario's Rice

Lake district. Atwood's historical vision of "explorers and ances-
tors" similarly approached the Canadian landscape in *Survival*
through a single point – with Susanna Moodie through the St.
Lawrence estuary. This approach echoed the journey of Northrop
Frye's archetypal traveller to Canada who

... enters into it like a tiny Jonah entering an inconceivably large whale, slip-
ping past the Strait of Belle Isle into the Gulf of St. Lawrence, where five
Canadian provinces surround him, for the most part invisible.... To enter the
United States is a matter of crossing an ocean; to enter Canada is a matter of
being swallowed by an alien continent.[10]

For Atwood, Canada is always Frye's whale, "unnamed" in "Progressive Insanities of the Pioneer," barely visible, ready to "swal-
low" those who do not attend to its hidden energies. The characters
in her fiction must descend into the whale to avoid being swallowed,
to transcend their alienation. In this descent the landscape often
becomes the wilderness of the character's unconscious, much as in
Frye the "vast unconsciousness of nature" becomes the inner "terror
of the soul" for the Canadian portrayed in literature.[11] To refuse to
be a victim, to refuse to be "swallowed by an alien continent," to
refuse to be alien to that continent and its mysteries, is also the message of *Survival* but again it pre-supposes Frye's vision – a harsh,
dwarfing land, a linear entry to the continent, an east-to-west vision
of cultural influence with the 'victim' sensibilities of the first settlers
arriving intact on the West Coast in the twentieth-century.
    The third difficulty *Survival* created for criticism lay in its ten-
dency to pass over writers who celebrated personal creativity, who
celebrated creativity as an essentially 'male' energy, or who failed to
perceive themselves or their characters as irredeemable victims. In a
sense, this tendency was part of the book's centralist vision, and of its
having inherited the Eastern-Canadian image of the land as – again
in Frye's words – "bleak and comfortless."[12] It may also have been
partly a consequence of Atwood's feminist perspective which, as we
have seen in her novels, locates creative energy in a wilderness that is
metaphorically female and which often mistrusts masculine energy
as being Adamic or manipulative. Left by Atwood to be restored to
the 'official' literature by other critics were such various writers as
Robertson Davies, Hugh Hood, Gwendolyn MacEwen, Daphne
Marlatt, Dorothy Livesay, bill bissett, bpNichol, Robert Kroetsch,
Irving Layton, and W.W.E. Ross, none of whose work presents
nature as alien or the self as defeated.

*

The basic premise of *Survival* was that Canadian writing has been characterized by "a preoccupation with ... survival ... with the obstacles to that survival" (33), and with "failure"; that

... at some point the failure to survive, or the failure to achieve anything beyond survival, becomes not a necessity imposed by a hostile outside world but a choice made from within. Pushed far enough, the obsession with surviving can become the will *not* to survive. (34)

The literature tends to portray characters who expect to be 'victims,' and reflects a country which sees itself as "a collective victim"(36). The most common form that such victimhood takes, Atwood suggests, is for the subject to acknowledge that he is a victim,

... but to explain this as an act of Fate, the Will of God, the dictates of Biology (in the case of women, for instance), the necessity decreed by History, or Economics, or the Unconscious, or any other large general powerful idea.

In any case, since it is the fault of this large *thing*, and not your own fault, you can neither be blamed for your position nor be expected to do anything about it. (37)

The body of the book illustrates from the literature specific images associated with the role of victimhood – nature as oppressive monster, North American Indians as either torturers or martyrs, explorers who find either nothing or death, families that serve mainly as traps for their members, immigrants who trade their ethnic past for bankruptcy and a non-existent 'Canadian identity,' artists who fail to create, and women who are "malevolent, or life-denying"(199).

While Atwood could sustain this interpretation of Canadian literature only through highly selective references to its texts, and while counter interpretations could doubtless be devised through equally selective choices of different texts, *Survival* today still serves two important functions. It continues to make Canadian literature interesting to non-literary audiences, and – more important to us here – provides important clues to the meaning of Atwood's own work.

*

Through the perspective of *Survival* the various non-communicative lovers of Atwood's poetry, lovers whose lives run parallel without touching, appear each to be holding the other responsible for the relationship, each believing that he or she should not "be expected to do anything about it." The male lover in "The Circle Game," is accused of enjoying posing as a victimized "orphan," "glad / to be left / out by himself in the cold" (*CG* 42). The lover of *Power Politics* who refuses "to own" himself is refusing to take responsibility for his own life. In fact, he views himself, the narrator suggests, as a kind of martyred Christ,

you ... walk towards me over the long floor

your arms outstretched, your heart
luminous through the ribs

around your head a crown
of shining blood (49)

Other figures in the poetry have bizarre expectations of the natural world. Some, like the younger sister in "Younger Sister, Going Swimming" narcissistically expect personal acknowledgement by nature. Others, like the pioneer of "Progressive Insanities" project the "monster" image of malevolence onto nature, casting it as 'victor' to their 'victim.' His initial assumption that a hostile nature must be suppressed by 'straight-line' human creations results, as Atwood herself notes in *Survival,* in his head being "invaded by the Nature which he has identified as chaos"(124). Susanna Moodie in *The Journals of Susanna Moodie* often shares the pioneer's paranoid feelings about nature, together with the conviction of the "younger sister" that the natural world owes her acknowledgement. However, she struggles against this sense of being abused by nature and toward personal responsibility for her feelings about the wilderness; "is it my own lack / of conviction which makes / these vistas of desolation"(11) she asks. It is this split which leads to her "double voice" – the first led by paranoia to construct self-protective lies about nature,

One [voice] had manners,
painted in watercolours,
used hushed tones when speaking
of mountains or Niagara Falls,
composed uplifting verse

and the second which acknowledges objective reality without feeling persecuted by it.

The other voice
had other knowledge:
that men sweat
always and drink often,
that pigs are pigs
but must be eaten
anyway, ... (42)

This distinction, between feeling victimized by natural events and
accepting such events as facts which one is obligated to cope with or
attempt to alter, is made equally clear in a pair of poems from *Two-
Headed Poems*. In the first, "The Woman Who Could Not Live with
her Faulty Heart," the woman feels separated from and abused by
her own body. She hears her heart as

... a constant pestering
in my ears, a caught moth, limping drum,
a child's fist beating
itself against the bedsprings
I want, I don't want.
How can one live with such a heart? (15)

In the second poem, "The Woman Makes Peace with her Faulty
Heart," the woman admits that it was not the "crippled rhythm" of
the heart which angered her but the way it "would not be captured"
or kept from "singing" its "raucous punctured song." At the conclusion she surrenders her victim role and accepts the unruly heart as her
own – "we're hooked / together like conspirators"(86-87).

Most of Atwood's short stories, which we surveyed in in the previous chapter, portray the condition of self-imposed victimhood rather
than a Susanna Moodie-like struggle to transcend it. The novels were
closely linked by Atwood to the victim theme in a 1972 interview,
made shortly after the publication of both *Survival* and *Surfacing*.
Here she expanded the discussion of 'victim' in *Survival* by defining
victimhood as a consequence of believing oneself innocent and of
believing an ideal "innocent" world to be attainable.

What I'm really into in that book [*Survival*] is the great Canadian victim
complex. If you define yourself as innocent, then nothing is ever your fault –
it is always somebody else doing it to you, and until you stop defining yourself as a victim, that will always be true. It will always be somebody else's
fault, and you will always be the object of that rather than somebody who
has any choice or takes responsibility for their life.

She also suggested that the narrator of *Surfacing*, in seeking to withdraw from all man-made structures and human contact, "wishes to be not human."

She wishes to be be not human, because being human inevitably involves being guilty, and if you define yourself as innocent, you can't accept that.[13]

We can see that this is also a pattern of behaviour in the other four novels. Marian MacAlpin withdraws from eating rather than be implicated in what she has subconsciously begun to experience as the reprehensible viciousness of mankind. Lesje in *Life Before Man* withdraws psychologically to a fantasy world of dinosaurs rather than face any share of responsibility for the events which have culminated in William's attempt to rape her. Rennie Wilford in *Bodily Harm* keeps all her relationships at a superficial level before learning in the Fort Industry prison that she is not "exempt" from human violence and love. In *Lady Oracle* Joan Foster engages in numerous flights from responsibility, deserting her first lover Paul without explanation, pretending suicide to escape the complications of her marriage, literary career, and affair with the Royal Porcupine. When she suspects the latter of threatening her life, she astonishingly blames not herself but her absent-minded husband for both the affair and the banality of their marriage.

... why had Arthur driven me to it, what did he propose to do about it, shouldn't we discuss our relationship to find out what had gone wrong? For some complicated and possibly sadistic reason of his own he'd allowed me to to become involved with a homicidal maniac, and it was time he knew about it. I didn't ask much, I only wanted to be loved. (272)

Her deepest wish is not for a responsible life in the everyday world but for a "pure" and innocent life in what she sees as the ideal world of the literary Gothic.

I longed for the simplicity of that world, where happiness was possible and wounds were only ritual ones. Why had I been closed out from that impossible white paradise where love was as final as death, and banished to this other place where everything changed and shifted. (284)

Both sides of her double vision of men as either killers or rescuers relieve her of any necessity to act for herself; she can be held responsible neither for her own death nor for her salvation.

Atwood pointed out when interviewed by Graeme Gibson in 1972 that such a belief in innocence leaves many afraid to "accept power" or to take "action" – "like people who refuse to get involved in politics because it's dirty."[14] They consequently abdicate responsibility for directing the course of their own lives. Passivity, the failure to act, is a characteristic not only of the central characters of all of Atwood's novels – as we saw in Chapter IV – but also of the supporting characters. Again these characters are marked by beliefs in impossible ideals or in their own innocence. In *The Edible Woman* Clara becomes involved in a "ridiculously idealistic" marriage to Joe; she greets "her first pregnancy with astonishment that it could happen to her"; burdened with three children she lapses into "inert fatalism"(36). She comes to view being a mother as being the victim of 'furtive' children who misbehave merely to persecute her. She says of her two-year old son,

'He just loves peeing behind doors. I wonder what it is. He's going to be secretive when he grows up, an undercover agent or a diplomat or something. The furtive little bastard.' (37)

In *Surfacing* the narrator's lover, Joe, feels similarly persecuted, like a "species once dominant, now threatened with extinction."

That's how he thinks of himself too: deposed, unjustly. Secretly he would like them to set up a kind of park for him, like a bird sanctuary. (8)

The narrator's father becomes out-of-touch with his daughter, not because he feels victimized, but because he believes himself innocent and insists on sustaining "his illusions of reason and benevolent order."(190) The order he and his wife create makes it impossible for his daughter to bring her real problems and feelings to them.

Their own innocence, the reason I couldn't tell them; perilous innocence, closing them in glass, their artificial garden, greenhouse. They didn't teach us about evil, they didn't understand about it, how could I describe it to them? (144)

In *Lady Oracle,* Arthur is another idealist whose beliefs lead him to feel victimized. Joan describes him as "a melancholy fighter for almost-lost causes, idealistic and doomed"(165). He has recurrent spells of "existential gloom;" he returns from Europe to Toronto to marry Joan because of "inertia and the absence of a sense of purpose"(196).

*

The most puzzling aspect of *Survival* is that it defies nearly all the injunctions against naming and categorization declared by Atwood's poetry and fiction. The author who objected to the utilitarianism of the "tourist center in Boston" and of Peter's "law books" and "marriage manuals" in *The Edible Woman* writes a "guide" to Canadian literature complete with a section entitled "How to Use this Book" and lists of "useful books." The author who disapproved of the pioneer's desire to 'name' the landscape attempts here to give a single name to an entire literature. *Survival* is also a systematically organized book: victimhood is analyzed into five basic "positions"; the survival theme itself is sub-divided into eleven "patterns." While nearly all modes of literary criticism have employed such second-order language (some exceptions are impressionistic, phenomenological and reader-response criticism), Atwood's approach in *Survival* exaggerates the critic's naming and classifying activities. With no visible sense of irony, the book embraces Joan Foster's faith in the efficacy of pattern, Peter's trust in *The Edible Woman* that generalizations can focus experience, Elizabeth's trust in *Life Before Man* that organization can create clarity and beauty.

Atwood's non-critical writing implies throughout that there could also be a truly female criticism – a non-instrumental use of critical language, a discontinuous and disjunctive argument, an iconic language of implication – possibly a critical structure of juxtaposed perceptions rather than of single linear argument. A decentralized literature like Canada's, in which geography transforms vision and individual writers see multiple and fluid realities in their own regions and create complex, multi-leveled structures – like Margaret Laurence's *The Diviners* – to acknowledge these realities, invites a critical approach that is 'liquid' rather than 'solid,' responsive rather than programmatic. Like the farm of "Progressive Insanities," Canadian literature needs an authentically Atwoodian approach – not a system of critical 'fences' but an ark that could float upon it.

CHAPTER NINE

# Epilogue

I believe that poetry is the heart of the language, the activity through which language is renewed and kept alive. I believe that fiction writing is the guardian of the moral and ethical sense of the community ... fiction is one of the few forms left through which we may examine our society not in its particular but in its typical aspects.
Margaret Atwood, "An End to Audience?"[1]

MARGARET Atwood's writing is an intriguing and engaging body of work – as I hope the preceding eight chapters imply. Like the best of modernist writing, Atwood's books are laconic, vivid, concrete in their imagery, disturbing in their juxtapositions. Like the best of contemporary writing, they combine a visible sense of play – pun, parody, self-parody, satire – with serious moral intent. Much of the pleasure offered by an Atwood text is literary, as in its deconstructions of the *Odyssey* in "Circe / Mud Poems," parodies of gothic romance in *Lady Oracle,* and ironic renderings of contemporary journalism in *Bodily Harm.*

Atwood's mistrust of "the received language" of conventional human speech, in fact, often leads her to create works that are gardens of textual delights. Almost all of her work has subtexts either implied or embedded within it – superhero stories, Shakespearean comedy, quest romance, descents to the underworld, television newscasts and commercials, billboards, horror movies. These subtexts, together with recurrent images, symbols, and narrative patterns constitute a 'female' sublanguage which rivals and often replaces discursive language. Atwood's work is thus ideally suited to a criticism which discounts declared meaning, which looks instead for sublanguages of syntax, vocabulary, literary structure, imagery, and symbol. A hidden advantage of such criticism – a considerable advantage when dealing with a living author as prolific as Atwood – is that such sublanguages tend to change, if at all, very slowly. In Atwood's case, for example, the sublanguage of *Bodily Harm* is essentially the same as that of *The Edible Woman* – a pseudo-comic narrative structure, a distrust of the spoken and written word, a descent to an underworld that affirms the instructive value of the Freudian unconscious, 'male' imagery of ropes, guns, cameras, books, knives, and cosmetics versus 'female' imagery of biology and intuition. The sublanguage readings provided here are thus unlikely to be quickly outdated by Atwood's subsequent work, and should provide an implicit reading of it.

*

Certainly there are aspects of Atwood's writing about which I have reservations; my approach throughout this book, however, has assumed that the writing and its languages should be identified and understood before any reservations about them are considered. Two questionable aspects of Atwood's writing for me are the female / male dichotomy implied by her imagery of underground and surface and the profound mistrust of men articulated in "Liking Men"(*MD* 53-54). Atwood's female / male metaphor not only tends to distort the nature of man and woman (except in *Life Before Man* Atwood rarely acknowledges any valuable rationalist elements in woman or primitive energy in man) but is only one of a number of possible analyses of the relationship between the primitive and the civilized. William Blake makes a similar analysis in *The Marriage of Heaven and Hell* (1790-93) in which he attempts to combine such antinomies as energy and restraint, passion and reason, Lion and Ox, joy and sanity, rebellion and orthodoxy. Like Atwood, he uses imagery that opposes the aboveground and the underground. Unlike her, he associates the underground with sexuality rather than a specific sex; unlike her also, he looks not for reconciliation and unsatisfactory compromise but for continuing and joyful struggle between the contending opposites. Charles Olson in his essay "Human Universe" (1958) is able to make Atwood's distinction between pre-rational and rational language without either denying speech or associating it with sexual difference. He too sees discursive speech as an enemy of passion and a distortion of natural process. His human universe, with its "language as the act of the instant" opposes a "universe of discourse" and its "language as the act of thought about the instant."[2] This human universe is specifically human rather than male or female; its rationalist other is characterized not by gender but by generalization.

In Canada, numerous writers have managed to articulate the conflict between sharply affirmative and defensive attitudes to life – between what Paul Bové has termed the "quest to escape nature and time" and the celebration of time[3] – without defining these attitudes as gender specific. Commenting on Atwood's "Progressive Insanities," D.G. Jones has argued in *Butterly on Rock* that "the only effective defense for a garrison culture is to abandon defense, to let down the walls and let the wilderness in, even to the wolves." For Jones, the terms of the conflict are "affirmation" versus "violence", openness versus closure; the advocates of affirmation include Leonard Cohen, Jay Macpherson, John Newlove, Anne Hébert, Douglas LePan, Gabrielle Roy and the writer from whose work the title of Jones' study is taken, Irving Layton.[4] Eli Mandel has recently argued that the metaphoric term for 'open' aesthetics should be 'west', that writers whose work is "popular, particularist in language, ... low or vulgar in approach, phenomenological in structure, discontinuous in form" (rather than "elitist, privileged ... formal in structure, continuous in form")[5] are "writing west".[6] The work of these writers, among whom he names bpNichol, bill bissett, Andy Suknaski, and Joe Rosenblatt, opposes the rational language of law and analysis with a "language of hallucination":

The language of hallucination, of disorientation, of irrationality has here become the means of a political statement, a vision of a whole people moving toward a world that, unlike ours, will know nothing of national corporations, technology, guns, or even civil order.[7]

Robert Kroetsch has offered a vision of 'ambiguity' in place of "extreme definition of male and female."

I've never thought of the erotic relationship as male aggression. It seems to me that it involves total exchange right to the freedom of who is aggressive, who is passive, who is doing what. I like that sense of ambiguity. Ambiguities make the erotic more complex.[8]

Kroetsch's fiction has the same repressive second-order language forces of rationalism and systematization (in his *Gone Indian* represented in Prof. Madham) as Atwood's; but Kroetsch suggests that one way to overcome these forces is through the liberation of the male and and his phallus. Kroetsch's central image for the liberation of the world from rationalism is the carnivalesque, with its phallic carnival king, Roger Dorck, in *Gone Indian* and the carnivalesque phallus of Johnny Backstrom in *The Words of My Roaring* that

breaks through both the ceremonial political language of Doc Murdoch and the 1935 Alberta drought, kindles lust in the doctor's
university-educated daughter, and even impregnates Johnny's tight-
lipped bride. Here the phallus belongs to men and women together,
and is roguish and sportive rather than bellicose.

Kroetsch shares Atwood's suspicion of language, but his suspect
language is that of history and *book*; such static literary language is
opposed for him not by the 'wordless' but by oral language –
Grizzly's language rather than William Dawe's field notes in *Badlands*, Jeremy's tape recordings rather than Prof. Madham's com-
mentaries in *Gone Indian*, Johnny Backstrom's chaotic speeches
rather than Doc Murdoch's rhetorical structures in *The Words of my
Roaring*. This dichotomy lets Kroetsch as a novelist embrace
language in its oral form rather than, like Atwood, write
ambivalently in a medium on which her own writing recurrently
casts doubt.

I also have reservations about the didactic tone that characterizes
much of Atwood's writing, its overt sense of deliberate patterning
and organization that often seems inimical to her endorsement of
irrational energies. Most of Atwood's fiction, in particular, seems
written at least in part to render a commentary on contemporary
society – in Atwood's own words, "to examine our society"; a character, she tells us, "fulfills ... a function" in a novel.[9] In this rationalist use of fiction the irrational properties of language, its unpredictable, undefinable and magical qualities, remain uninvoked; a certain
predictability of image, symbol, and structure is unavoidably
created. It is this magical quality that Carolyn Forché, reviewing for
*The New York Times Book Review,* found lacking in Atwood's
*Selected Poems.*

It is lamentable that her voice so often indulges itself, meandering through
these narratives with a stridency and submission to intention that preclude
any power of language itself to issue its mysteries.
    ... reading these poems is like following the maps she so much wishes des-
troyed. (21 May 1978, p. 42)

In such a reading of Atwood, her work becomes one of Eli Mandel's
self-reflexive "strange loops,"[10] – a writing written against its own
writing, a writing that denies its writer. That is, the rationalist that
Atwood opposes in her writing, the manipulative, amputating,
technology-using, analyzing figure of glass and marble becomes to
some extent herself – clever writer, witty satirist, a Rennie Wilford,

too much in control of a specific language pattern to let language speak its own words even as she asks it to so speak.

One senses in the various portraits of writers in her work a self-reflexive declaration – that she would step away from her own recurrent patterns of images, that she would, as Eli Mandel suggests, "write west" into the body of the language, into the language as itself an underworld which is mysterious and life-giving. But she may be held by her own definitions. Having defined conventional language not as underground, Derridian mystery but as a tool of rationalism, she may be excluded from the mystery she has denied. Having defined the underworld in terms of Frye's image for the Canadian landscape, Leviathan, and having further defined it as female, she cannot stay within it but must keep returning to rationalism for both 'safety' and sexual completion. Hence the two dilemmas of Atwood's female protagonists – to live, as in *Surfacing* between the alternatives of dangerous wilderness and dangerous city; or, as in *Murder in the Dark,* to need "desperately" to like men who have become by definition "enemy."

... just because all rapists are men it doesn't follow that all men are rapists, you tell yourself. You try desperately to retain the image of the man you love and also like, but now it's a sand-coloured plain, no houses left standing anywhere, columns of smoke ascending, trenches filled with no quarter, heads the faces rotting away, mothers, babies, young boys and girls, men as well, turning to skulls, who did this? Who defines *enemy?* How can you like men? ("Liking Men," *MD* 54)

*

In some of Atwood's recent writing there are hints of dissatisfaction with old idioms and fascination with new. In Part II of *Murder in the Dark* Atwood offers four miniature 'novels' – "Women's Novels," "Happy Endings," "Bread," and "The Page." In appearance these are prose poems, separated into discrete stanzas by sequential numbers, letters, or by single asterisks. The most interesting feature of these 'novels' is their disjunctive structure. Each stanza begins the story over again, offers an alternative version to the stories of the earlier stanzas. In "Women's Novels" each stanza implies a different fiction, "men's novels about men," "novels in which the heroine has a costume rustling discretely over her breasts," novels with "happiness guaranteed, joy all round, covers with nurses on them"(35-36); some stanzas imply multiple fictions. "Happy Endings" offers different plots for the same characters.

A. John and Mary fall in love and get married. They both have worthwhile and remunerative jobs which they find stimulating ....

B. Mary falls in love with John but John doesn't fall in love with Mary. He merely uses her body....

C. John, who is an older man, falls in love with Mary, and Mary, who is only twenty-two, feels sorry for him.... (37-38)

The poems thus become parodies of plot and structure that reverse the reliance on a single recurrent narrative pattern that characterizes Atwood's 'comic' novels, become unstated criticisms of those novels. As single units, the poems become metafictions, works that simultaneously create fictions and comment on their own creations.

The language of these prose poems is dense, subtle, and playful – quite unlike the wordiness of some of her novels. Syntax receives such emphasis that it becomes content.

5. The question about the page is: what is beneath it? It seems to have only two dimensions, you can pick it up and turn it over and the back is the same as the front. Nothing, you say, disappointed.

But you were looking in the wrong place, you were looking *on the back* instead of *beneath*. *Beneath the page* is another story. Beneath the page is a story. Beneath the page is everything that has ever happened, most of which you would rather not hear about.

The page is not a pool but a skin, a skin is there to hold in and it can feel you touching it. Did you really think it would just lie there and do nothing?

Touch the page at your peril: it is you who are blank and innocent, not the page. (45)

These prose poems appear to explore much more resonant fictional modes than Atwood has attempted previously. In their metafictional aspects they offer a way simultaneously to offer a fiction such as Marian MacAlpin's story and to comment ironically upon it, or to offer alternative versions of questionable stories. In their foregrounding of syntax they appear to offer a way to bring to the novel the linguistic playfulness and complexity of Atwood's poetry.

The disjunctive or alternative quality of the poems is repeated in the hypotheticality of another recent Atwood fiction, the children's story "The Festival of Missed Crass."[11] Although there are occasional hints of an atomic apocalypse throughout Atwood's writing ("The End of the World: Weekend, near Toronto," *PU* 32; "When it Happens," *DG* 125-137) and corresponding hints of science fiction,

"The Festival of Missed Crass" is Atwood's only firm step into fiction of the hypothetical future. The story is set in Toronto some centuries after an atomic war, where a society of stolid underground people, the "Furts," have managed to survive in the ruins of subway tunnels. The rules and prohibitions of this society, however, which evolved during a time when lethal radiation awaited anyone who ventured to the surface, have become obsolete now that this radiation has subsided and new surface life-forms have grown. Here the familiar Atwood theme of closed, dogmatic behaviour versus evolving life is evident, although with an ironic reversal – 'underground' is now the home of convention, surface the realm of change. The Furts have descended into the Virgilian underworld for safety and instruction, but have forgotten to resurface; for them underworld consequently becomes the static kingdom of their "Eldurts" who "plug" open tunnels and punish rule-breaking by imprisoning the offender in a "cyst." Within Atwood's vocabulary of symbols and images, to "plug" a burrow or tunnel (compare the soldiers in "Spelling" [TS 63] who tie the legs together of a woman in labour) is an act categorically hostile to both process and woman.

But the focus of "The Festival of Missed Crass" falls not on characters who deny change but on Plogula, a small girl who defies the social paralysis of her people to walk out to the new surface world. Here she is welcomed by Sympleni, a descendant of one of a number of Furts who have preceded her and who have evolved into 'Plena' (presumably from the Latin plenus, 'full'), a people who value a full life that embraces both custom and change. "Honour to those who risk," he says to Plogula in welcome. Later he tells her the Plena are "creatures of custom like the Furts, but we like to know what our customs mean." On the surface she also finds trees returning, and "Changers," the transparent survivors of the first Furts to manage to survive above ground.

One can read "The Festival of Missed Crass" as an 'optimistic' parable of the deconstruction of a language-bound civilization to allow the birth of a poetic, fluid world of Changers who metamorphose continuously from human, to plant, to bird, and who "whatever they become" sing. The names of Toronto's subway stations have collapsed into new words, Union Station has become "NION SAION," Dundas has become "UNDAS"; the language overall has liquified old spellings and pronunciations: Myrtle has become "Murdle," Simpson's Basement has become "IMPSONS BASM," sewer-rat has become "soo-rat," school has become "grool," garbage *bucket* has become "garbukki," the Furt's staple diet of fungus has become "fung." Plogula herself, on coming to the surface and "soon-light," metamorphoses from grey-skinned Furt to pink-skinned "Wimpi."

Perhaps one can also read "The Festival of Missed Crass" as a hypothetical Atwood portrait of a better world, where "crass" has been eliminated from 'Christmas,' where custom and change have become combined harmoniously in human creation, where custom itself is meaningful rather than mechanical, and where language is no longer a masculine Adamic imposition on the world but an harmonious analogue to it. For among the Plena are "Wordhoarders," whose job

is first to preserve whatever meanings we can; and if we can't do that, we try to restore the words whose meanings have become blurred or damaged by giving them new meanings. 'Wordorder is Worldorder,' we say.

The Wordhoarders thus work to prevent first-order language from becoming second-order language, and thus to prevent ritual actions whose purpose "nobody knows anymore. That's what happens when the meanings of words are lost."

Saplissa, the Plena's female Wordhoarder who speaks above, is a kind of Atwood self-portrait, a poet who in the tradition of Arnold and Pound sees herself as a custodian of language and culture, a protector and renewer of meanings. "Wordorder is Worldorder" illuminates the extraordinary focus of Atwood's novels on language, on the role of language in cultural health, and on protagonists who use language with either precision or imprecision. The troubles of the world, from the love problems of "The Circle Game" to the political upheavals of *Bodily Harm*, are all in a sense linguistic problems that stem from Adamic language and its arbitrary and distorting imposition on experience. In Atwood's post-atomic and post-Adamic world (the nuclear bomb being perhaps the ultimate phallic weapon) the Wordhoarder is notably female, and language has become metaphorically the world.

# Notes

## CHAPTER ONE: An Unneeded Biography

1 Linda Sandler, "Interview with Margaret Atwood," *The Malahat Review,* No. 41, January 1977, p. 16.
2 "Travels Back," *Maclean's,* January 1973, p. 28.
3 Sandler, p. 14.
4 Graeme Gibson, "Margaret Atwood" (interview), *Eleven Canadian Novelists* (Toronto: House of Anansi, 1973), p. 17.
5 Sandler, p. 10.
6 Joyce Carol Oates, "An Interview with Margaret Atwood," *The New York Times Book Review,* May 21, 1978, p. 15.
7 Gibson, p. 11.
8 Gibson, pp. 11-12.
9 See Marci McDonald, "A New Literary Star Emerges in Canadian Letters," *The Toronto Star,* October 21, 1972, p. 77.
10 James Ayre, "Margaret Atwood and the End of Colonialism," *Saturday Night* 87, November 1972, pp. 23-26.
11 See William French, "Icon and Target: Atwood as Thing," *The Globe and Mail,* April 7, 1973, p. 28.
12 Sandler, p. 9.
13 Quoted in Roy MacGregor, "Atwood's World," *Maclean's,* October 15, 1979, p. 64.
14 Sandler, p. 26.
15 Sandler, p. 14.
16 Sandler, p. 22.

## CHAPTER TWO: Poetry of Male and Female Space

1 *The White Goddess* (New York: Vintage, 1960 [1948]), pp. 515-525. See also *Pausanias's Description of Greece,* translated with a commentary by James Frazer (London: Macmillan, 1913), Vol. 5, pp. 234-239.
2 (New York: New American Library, 1947 [1938]).
3 (London: Chatto and Windus, 1956).
4 *Man in the Modern Age,* tr. Eden and Cedar Paul (New York: Doubleday Anchor, 1951 [1931]), pp. 5-6.
5 "Foreword: *Periods of the Moon,*" *Engagements* (Toronto: McClelland and Stewart, 1972), pp. 124-126.
6 "Preface: *The Laughing Rooster,*" *Engagements,* p. 114.

## CHAPTER THREE: The Insufficiency of Poetry

1 "Timeless Constructions," *The Malahat Review* 41, January 1977, pp. 107-120.
2 "Atwood Gothic," *The Malahat Review* 41, January 1977, p. 174.

CHAPTER FOUR: Four Female 'Comedies'

1 "The Dark Voyage: *The Edible Woman* as Romance," in Arnold E. Davidson and Cathy N. Davidson, ed., *The Art of Margaret Atwood* (Toronto: House of Anansi, 1981), p. 125.
2 "*Surfacing* and the Rebirth Journey," in *The Art of Margaret Atwood*, p. 151.
3 "Descent and Return in 'Surfacing'," in Rigney's *Madness and Sexual Politics in the Feminist Novel: Studies in Brontë, Woolf, Lessing and Atwood* (Madison, Wis.: University of Wisconsin Press, 1978), pp. 114-115.

CHAPTER SIX: An Atwood Vocabulary

1 *Alphabet* 10, July 1962, pp. 78-79.
2 J. R. Struthers, "An Interview with Margaret Atwood," *Essays in Canadian Writing* 6, Spring 1977, p. 25.
3 See Margaret A. Murray, *The God of the Witches* (London: Oxford University Press, 1970 [1931]).
4 "An Essay on Pan," *Pan and the Nightmare* (New York: Spring Publications, 1972), p. xxii.
5 *The White Goddess* (New York: Vintage Press, 1960 [1948]), pp. 424-454.
6 Linda Sandler, "Interview with Margaret Atwood," *The Malahat Review*, No. 41, January 1977, p. 16.
7 Struthers, *ibid.*, p. 21.
8 Graeme Gibson, *Eleven Canadian Novelists* (Toronto: House of Anansi, 1973), p. 25.

CHAPTER EIGHT: *Survival:* The Victim Theme

1 Marci McDonald, "A New Literary Star Emerges in Canadian Letters," *The Toronto Star*, October 21, 1972, p. 77.
2 November 4, 1972, p. 79.
3 October 28, 1972, p. 33.
4 Christopher Driver, "Hastings Owl," *The Listener* 14, March 1974, pp. 342-343.
5 October 1972, pp. 10-11.
6 *The Malahat Review* 26, April 1973, pp. 233-234.
7 January 1973, pp. 32-33.
8 Walter E. Swayze, "Survey and Survival," *Journal of Canadian Fiction*, III: 1 (Winter 1974), 112-113.
9 "Conclusion," *The Literary History of Canada* (Toronto: University of Toronto Press, 1965), p. 821.
10 *Ibid.*, p. 824.
11 *Ibid.*, p. 830.
12 *Ibid.*
13 Graeme Gibson, *Eleven Canadian Novelists* (Toronto: House of Anansi, 1973), p. 22.
14 *Ibid.*, p. 24.

CHAPTER NINE: Epilogue

1 *Dalhousie Review*, LX:3 (Autumn 1980), p. 424.
2 *Evergreen Review*, II:5 (Summer 1958), p. 89. Reprinted in Charles Olson, *Human Universe and other Essays* (New York: Grove Press, 1967), pp. 3-15.
3 *Destructive Poetics* (New York: Columbia University Press, 1980).
4 (Toronto: University of Toronto Press, 1970), pp. 8-9.

5   "Strange Loops: Northrop Frye and Cultural Freudianism," *Canadian Journal of Political and Social Theory*, V:3, (Fall 1981), p. 33.

6   "Writing West: on the Road to Wood Mountain," *Another Time* (Erin, Ont.: Press Porcepic, 1977), pp. 68-78.

7   "Ecological Heroes and Visionary Politics," *Another Time*, p. 111.

8   Shirley Neuman and Robert Wilson, *Labyrinths of Voice: Conversations with Robert Kroetsch* (Edmonton: NeWest Press, 1982), p. 24.

9   "PCR Interview with Margaret Atwood," *Poetry Canada Review*, I:4 (1980), p. 8.

10   "Strange Loops: Northrop Frye and Cultural Freudianism," p. 33.

11   *Chatelaine*, LII:12 (December 1979), 44-45, 84, 86, 90, 92, 94-95.

# Bibliography

## Works by Margaret Atwood

POETRY

*Double Persephone*. Toronto: Hawkshead Press, 1961.
*The Circle Game*. Toronto: Contact Press, 1966.
*The Animals in That Country*. Toronto: Oxford University Press, 1968.
*The Journals of Susanna Moodie*. Toronto: Oxford University Press, 1970.
*Procedures for Underground*. Toronto: Oxford University Press, 1970.
*Power Politics*. Toronto: Oxford University Press, 1971.
*You Are Happy*. Toronto: Oxford University Press, 1974.
*Selected Poems*. Toronto: Oxford University Press, 1976.
*Two-Headed Poems*. Toronto: Oxford University Press, 1978.
*True Stories*. Toronto: Oxford University Press, 1981.
*Murder in the Dark*. Toronto: The Coach House Press, 1982.
*Interlunar*. Toronto: Oxford University Press, 1984.

FICTION

*The Edible Woman*. Toronto: McClelland and Stewart, 1969.
*Surfacing*. Toronto: McClelland and Stewart, 1972.
*Lady Oracle*. Toronto: McClelland and Stewart, 1976.
*Dancing Girls*. Toronto: McClelland and Stewart, 1977.
*Life Before Man*. Toronto: McClelland and Stewart, 1979.
*Bodily Harm*. Toronto: McClelland and Stewart, 1981.
*Bluebeard's Egg*. Toronto: McClelland and Stewart, 1983.

OTHER PROSE

*Survival: a Thematic Guide to Canadian Literature*. Toronto: House of Anansi, 1972.
"Grace Marks." Unpublished playscript, 1974, 85 pp. [Produced on CBC Television in January 1974 as *The Servant Girl*.]

*Days of the Rebels: 1815-1840.* Canada's Illustrated Heritage series.
Toronto: McClelland and Stewart, 1977.
*Second Words* (essays). Toronto: House of Anansi, 1983.

Selected Criticism

Bowering, George, "Margaret Atwood's Hands," *Studies in Canadian Literature,* VI:1 (1981), 39-52.
Brown, Russell M. "Atwood's Sacred Wells," *Essays in Canadian Writing* 17, Spring 1980, pp. 5-43.
Christ, Carol P., "Margaret Atwood: the Surfacing of Women's Spiritual Quest and Vision," *Signs: Journal of Women in Culture and Society,* II: 2 (1976), 331-339.
Davidson, Arnold E. and Cathy N. "The Anatomy of Margaret Atwood's *Surfacing,*" *Ariel,* X:3 (July 1979), 38-54.
————. "Margaret Atwood's *Lady Oracle:* the Artist as Escapist and Seer," *Studies in Canadian Literature,* III:2 (Summer 1978), 166-177.
————. "Prospects and Retrospects in *Life Before Man,*" in Davidson and Davidson, ed., *The Art of Margaret Atwood* (Toronto: House of Anansi, 1981), pp. 205-222.
Foster, John Wilson. "The Poetry of Margaret Atwood," *Canadian Literature* 74, Autumn 1977, pp. 5-20.
Grace, Sherrill. *Violent Duality: a Study of Margaret Atwood.* Montreal: Véhicule Press, 1980.
Johnston, Gordon. " 'The Ruthless Story and the Future Tense' in Margaret Atwood's 'Circe / Mud Poems,' " *Studies in Canadian Literature,* V:1 (Spring 1980), 167-176.
Lecker, Robert. "Janus through the Looking Glass: Atwood's First Three Novels," in Davidson and Davidson, ed., *The Art of Margaret Atwood,* pp. 177-204.
Mandel, Eli. "Atwood Gothic," *The Malahat Review* 41, January 1977, pp. 165-174.
Mansbridge, Francis. "Search for Self in the Novels of Margaret Atwood," *Journal of Canadian Fiction* 22, 1978, pp. 106-117.
Marshall, Tom. "Atwood Over and Above Water," *The Malahat Review* 41, January 1977, pp. 89-94.
McLay, Catherine. "The Dark Voyage: *The Edible Woman* as Romance," in Davidson and Davidson, ed., *The Art of Margaret Atwood,* pp. 123-138.

Pratt, Annis. "*Surfacing* and the Rebirth Journey," in Davidson and Davidson, ed., *The Art of Margaret Atwood,* pp. 139-158.

Rigney, Barbara Hill. "Descent and Return in *Surfacing,*" in her *Madness and Sexual Politics in the Feminist Novel: Studies in Brontë, Woolf, Lessing, and Atwood* (Madison, Wis.: University of Wisconsin Press, 1978), pp. 91-127.

Rule, Jane. "Life, Liberty, and the Pursuit of Normalcy – the Novels of Margaret Atwood," *The Malahat Review* 41, January 1977, pp. 42-49.

Skelton, Robin. "Timeless Constructions – a Note on the Poetic Style of Margaret Atwood," *The Malahat Review* 41, January 1977, pp. 107-120.

Sullivan, Rosemary. "*Surfacing* and *Deliverance,*" *Canadian Literature* 67, Winter 1976, pp. 6-20.

## Interviews

Gibson, Graeme. "Margaret Atwood," in his *Eleven Canadian Novelists.* Toronto: House of Anansi, 1973, pp. 1-31.

Oates, Joyce Carol. "An Interview with Margaret Atwood," *New York Times Book Review,* 21 May 1978, pp. 15, 43-45.

PCR. "Interview with Margaret Atwood," *Poetry Canada Review,* I:4 (1980), 8, 10.

Sandler, Linda. "Interview with Margaret Atwood," *The Malahat Review* 41, January 1977, pp. 7-27.

Schiller, William. "Interview with Margaret Atwood," *Poetry Windsor Poésie,* II:3 (Fall 1976), 2-15.

Struthers, J.R. "An Interview with Margaret Atwood," *Essays in Canadian Writing* 6, Spring 1977, pp. 18-27.

## Bibliographic Surveys

Horne, Alan J. "Margaret Atwood: an Annotated Bibliography (Prose)," in Robert Lecker and Jack David, ed., *The Annotated Bibliography of Canada's Major Authors,* Vol. I (Downsview, Ont.: ECW Press, 1979), 13-46.

————. "Margaret Atwood: an Annotated Bibliography (Poetry,)" in *The Annotated Bibliography of Canada's Major Authors,* Vol. II (Downsview, Ont.: ECW Press, 1980), 13-53.

————. "Margaret Atwood: a Checklist of Writings by and about," in Davidson and Davidson, *The Art of Margaret Atwood,* pp. 243-285.

# Index